Violence and the Cultural Politics of Trauma

Violence and the Cultural Politics of Trauma

Jane Kilby

Edinburgh University Press

© Jane Kilby, 2007

Edinburgh University Press Ltd
22 George Square, Edinburgh

Typeset in 11/13pt Ehrhardt MT
by Servis Filmsetting Ltd, Manchester, and
printed and bound in Great Britain by
Biddles Ltd, King's Lynn, Norfolk

A CIP record for this book is available from the British Library

ISBN 978 0 7486 1816 3 (hardback)

Contents

Preface: Putting it Lightly: The History and Future of Speaking Out About Violence

In 1978, when Louise Armstrong wrote *Kiss Daddy Goodnight* 'as a first-person, documentary book on incest' (1978: 15), she was among the first radical feminists and victims of sexual abuse to find herself speaking publicly about the experience of incest. Based on her own testimony as well as the letters and conversations with the survivors who had responded to her advertisement for help, *Kiss Daddy Goodnight* was the first book drawing on women's testimony to 'break the silence' that had governed the reality of sexual abuse, which is to say it was the first book to actively challenge the myths that had dominated understanding of incest whereby it was typically thought of as a benign experience if not a mutually informed experience born from victim complicity. There was not an incest taboo, it was argued at the time, but there was a taboo on speaking about it as a violent reality sustained by the power men held over women and children. Giving personal testimony to the violence of incest became the politics of the day, with Armstrong, like other radical feminists at the time, convinced that it would institute unprecedented change. Revolution was in the air and for this reason *Kiss Daddy Goodnight* was written with a sense of profound hope. It was also buoyed by a lively sense of humour and a surprising degree of levity. At times, it can make you laugh, but not always.

But when updating the book for its tenth anniversary edition Armstrong's tone changes considerably. 'Dear Reader,' she writes in 1987, 'I approach this re-introduction of *Kiss Daddy Goodnight* with, if anything, a greater sense of urgency than the original publication ten years ago' (1987: vii). 'True,' she continues, things seemed pretty bad when I first began listening to women who been molested as children within the family. True, also, that the more I listened, the worse the *stories* I heard. However, since we first spoke out, I have watched the situation become almost unimaginably horrific. (ibid.: vii)

A short decade after she spoke out, Armstrong is already expressing a creeping dismay due, she argues, to the unexpected growth of an 'incest industry', an amorphous amalgam of state-sponsored and private sector 'problem-management' programmes which, because they were psychotherapeutically or otherwise medically informed, focused on the individual, and on the individual alone. It was not the change that Armstrong had expected, which is why she ends up in 1987 reckoning that it had not been the intention of radical feminists to 'merely' start 'a long conversation' about incest (ibid.: ix). 'We hoped to raise hell. We hoped to raise change. What we raised, it would seem, was discourse' (ibid.: ix).

By the time that she writes *Rocking the Cradle of Sexual Politics* in 1994 Armstrong's concern has grown to such a degree that she is maintaining that as 'a political story' speaking out about incest has become 'a prime illustration of how it is now possible for the powers-that-be to use *noise* to achieve the same end that was once served by repression' (1994: 3). She then proceeds to paint a distinctly cynical picture, holding the success of 'incest industry' responsible for why in only a short number of years we had gone 'from enforced secrecy, the suppression of children's experiences, women's experiences, such that they were not ever heard – to a level of cacophony such that children's voices, women's voices, are once more not, in any purposeful way, being heard' (ibid.: 7-8). Indeed, for Armstrong 'the vampirish mental health maw' of the psychotherapeutically informed incest industry 'drains meaning from the words it puts mouth to before sending them forth to do its work' (ibid.: 30). Psychotherapeutic discourse thus emerges as a profound panacea, with Armstrong seriously doubting the 'new freedom to speak' being enjoyed by women (ibid.: 76). Paradoxically, then, the legacy of a feminist politics of speaking out is both 'noise' and 'a kind of aphasia: a loss of words, the material of speech itself' (ibid.: 208). In light of this appraisal, Armstrong concludes that 'breaking the silence has now become an end in itself' (ibid.: 205), with little or no opportunity for discussing the 'larger meaning' of sexual exploitation. 'A new veil of silence' has descended, she argues, 'woven of a magical new hi-tech fabric. This fabric is permeable by the personal, but it [acts] as a filter, blocking out the political' and all that gets through, she laments, is '*stories*: battered women's *stories*, rape victims' *stories*, incest victims' *stories*' (ibid.: 76). Little wonder, then, that Armstrong ends her analysis reflecting on the fact that she finds optimism a struggle.

I have chosen to preface my book with Armstrong's rolling account of the politics of speaking out because it set the questions for the writing of *Violence and the Cultural Politics of Trauma*, a project I began in the mid-1990s just after the publication of her final commentary and amid the rhetorical fallout of the false memory syndrome debates. The questions as I understood them at the time and still do (if admittedly now articulated with greater acuity) are: how might we think about breaking this 'new veil of silence', and is it as radically different as Armstrong implies? What is the purpose of listening to women's testimony, and might there not be politically alternative ways of listening? Are words so easily exhausted, redirected and recuperated? Is the new freedom to speak only a function of the incest industry? Are words, in fact, the material of speech? Why does talking for the sake of talking figure as a political dead end? Is it not possible to figure conversation as a political form? What, indeed, is the larger meaning of incest and does politics require meaning as such? Does anything have the power to completely block out testimony? And finally, if not most importantly: how do you inherit a politics when those who began it have lost hope in the project?

In asking and answering these questions throughout this book, it is not my intention to simply critique radical feminists, such as Armstrong, by mobilising post-structuralist insights concerning the relationship of language and power. Thus, for example, my position differs from that held by the editors of the recent *New Feminist Stories of Child Sexual Abuse: Sexual Scripts and Dangerous Dialogues*, who

> draw on recent developments in post-structuralist theory to enable a
> more critical reading of women and child sexual abuse: to do more

than simply articulate women's experiences but to theorise why particular experiences are raised or ignored and what institutions and
institutional practices these invite and sustain. (Reavey and Warner
2003: 5)

For while their project is a necessary condition for thinking through
the politics of speaking out about child sexual abuse, it is not, I would
contend, a sufficient one. (Nor, I might add, do I think it is as theoretically daring or risky as they suggest.) It is not adequate in the sense
that when feminists rely on the insights of post-structuralism alone,
the analytical privileging of institutions and their incitatory discourses is achieved at the expense of a consideration of experience
itself, which is typically bracketed or else put aside - in this instance,
as a matter of the seemingly already known task of having to 'simply
articulate women's experiences'. I should stress here that I am not
looking to establish an unmediated theory of victim experience as
such, but rather I am keen to argue that women's experiences of child
sexual abuse are more difficult to express theoretically than Reavey
and Warner appear to suggest here. Thereby the aim of this book is to
provide a sustained engagement with the phenomenon of victim
experience, an engagement that will require an understanding of the
textuality of women's testimony to sexual violence, but an analysis,
nonetheless, that is not dictated by the terms of post-structuralism
(such that is possible to figure the challenge of articulating women's
experiences as somehow critically retrograde).

While Reavey and Warner suggest that post-structuralism offers
an advance or at least an alternative to radical feminist thinking on
women's experiences of incest, it is nonetheless important to stress
that radical feminists were not expressly concerned with theorizing
the experience of violence per se, focusing instead on how the reality
of sexual abuse was hidden as a truth for countless women and children. Indeed, it is possible to argue that there has been continuing
failure to analyse the trauma of incest, even though it was a question
for radical feminism from the start. For when Armstrong wrote *Kiss
Daddy Goodnight* she asked questions about the experience, possible
trauma and survival of incest:

What were our feelings at the time? Later? Did we have common
stages of recovery? How many of us had managed to seal the

experience off in a tomb? Could anyone do that forever? Or did it always breed enough noxious gas to explode? Was it, ever, a neutral experience? Was the effect related to the degree of assault? (1978: 15)

These are important questions that suggest an understanding of the impact of violence and the complexity of victim experience. But she heard it from others as well. Indeed, Armstrong's key correspondent – a woman called Jenny - confirms that for a large part of her adult life she had 'no awareness' that anything 'had happened' because she had 'completely removed it from any form of consciousness' (ibid.: 23). Clearly, then, Armstrong knew it to be a question, and when in quiet, intimate conversation with Jenny she would be careful of her trauma:

'Look, Jenny,' I'd say. 'I don't want to push you.' 'No, really,' she'd say. 'I just have to make myself do it. It'll just take a little time.' 'Well. Maybe you'll find it's not so bad as you think. Words don't bite.' 'No. They just nibble a little.' (ibid.: 22)

Taking place in 1978 this was a conversation rich with an understanding of the struggle to articulate the painful reality of incest, of the time needed and how, in the final analysis, testifying can bring its own trauma. Thus right from the beginning there was a recognition that trauma is part of the experience of incest and that it has a complicated relationship to (the power of) language.

Crucially, however, it was a private conversation and the recognition remained private. In public, Armstrong refused the trauma question whenever it was addressed to her. Indeed, as Armstrong makes expressly clear she has always

passed through (dodged, if you prefer) [the scarred forever] question and back to the power abuse. ('Obviously, rape by someone you are meant to trust is acutely painful, but what the women I listened to were more hurt by was the social permission, the license . . .'). (1994: 34)

So rather than address the questions that might flow from her recognition of the relationship between trauma and language - which was politically significant at the time given the tendency to minimise the harm caused by sexual abuse – Armstrong shifted the terms of analysis away from the psychic impact of incest to an interrogation of power, its misuse and its reproduction.

Of course, Armstrong had good reasons for shifting the debate away from the trauma caused by incest, not least being her sense of the commercial and prurient interest generated by the possibility of sexual, psychic wounding, and ultimately, as she understood it, the conservative consequences of focusing on personal pain. 'By 1984', she argues, 'the very meaning of incest had been changed: the noun *incest* had become a verb: "I was incested when I was five" (which sounded sort of like, "I was baptized when I was five")' (ibid.: 97). While Armstrong is being distinctly harsh here, the point remains: naming oneself a victim of incest had become the mark of deep and profoundly held identity. And as a consequence the politics of incest 'evolved into [. . .]: a pain competition, a victimization sweepstakes, a demand that the political, which had emerged from overwhelming commonalities, be denied in deference to the perfectly genuine pain of the personal' (ibid.: 62-3). In keeping with critics then, Armstrong considers the very personal nature of trauma to be politically detrimental. If trauma is to serve as a political commentary on violence, her reasoning goes, it must move beyond personal experience: strategically, if paradoxically, the pain has to be taken out of the story.

The aim of *Violence and the Cultural Politics of Trauma* is to put it (back) into the story, not least because while I admire Armstrong's commentary it is overly deterministic and reductive, especially when parodying women today who choose to have the kind of conversation she had with Jenny but with a therapist, an on-line survivor or talk show host. And while Armstrong would hardly contemplate that she was the only incest survivor 'in the world' as she did in 1978 – a 'morbid thought' (1978: 15) – there is also little point in her continuing to figure political change and sociality in the twenty-first century in the likeness of her own rational response to the scarred-forever question. Things really have changed, as she knows only too well, and while the lessons to be learnt are still open to debate, it is clear that a politics built on a logical exploration of the permission given men to abuse children and women is not enough to secure a transformed future. Today women are more intent on discussing the acutely painful nature of the incest experience itself, rather, it seems, than exploring their pain in the politically instrumental terms suggested by Armstrong. Thus feminism requires a theoretically robust language for engaging with, rather than dismissing, all this trauma talk, and on this score I warrant that feminism has nothing to lose by borrowing from the psychotherapeutic and psychoanalytic languages of the incest industry; and while Armstrong is right to point up the frequently ameliorating individualism of such discourses of trauma, this is not a binding condition of their subsequent use. Thus I intend to draw on the language of trauma to put victim experience back into the feminist story of speaking out, and when I say put the pain back into the story I mean that as literally as it can be read; put less obliquely, if feminism is going to accommodate the experience of incest it will have to be undone by trauma, a condition that will also apply to feminists who draw on psychoanalysis and other psychotherapeutic/psychodynamic models. This said, however, there is more than one way to read trauma back into the story of politics.

Inspired by the recent developments in trauma and testimony theory – especially the work of Cathy Caruth – my aim in this book is to suggest that trauma theory provides the necessary language and reading skills to produce a different political story, a story not tied to the individual as such nor a story told in the general terms of gender, patriarchy and power. Admittedly, given that Caruth is a literary and psychoanalytic theorist who is clearly indebted to the insights and methods of deconstruction, trauma theory seems an unlikely resource and I am sure that Armstrong would not be convinced by my efforts. Importantly, however, and as unlikely as it seems, Armstrong and Caruth share a vital thing in common, if understanding and thereby valuing it in different ways. Both place, I would argue, a premium on the ability of language to transcend its conditions of possibility. For Caruth, then, language cannot translate the experience of trauma as manifest meaning: it is unrepresentable. But while Caruth understands unrepresentability to be the condition of possibility for victim testimony, this alone does not cancel its force or indeed the possibility of witnessing. It is simply that the power of language is not reducible to its ability to represent.

In contrast to Caruth, Armstrong has never in theory expressed any concern over the limits of representation or the formal conditions of language, but as a practicing journalist she demonstrates a keen sense of how the power of language works beyond its ability to express meaning. Let me explain. In the context of her experience of incest, Armstrong's use of the phrase '*Kiss Daddy Goodnight*' works to signify something other than an innocuous request. By reciting her father's words in an entirely different context, Armstrong is able to expose their power to silence her (how can anyone object to such a request?). In this instance, language has to give up some of its power. As reported speech '*Kiss Daddy Goodnight*' works to rewrite its conditions of intelligibility, and as a consequence language is made to answer for its power to silence, to report back. In this way, Armstrong is seizing the power of her father's discourse and having the last say. And she is having her last say with the humour that he used to silence her with – 'You know, for someone with a sense of humour you're being awfully gloomy. The trouble with most of you women is you just won't admit that at fourteen you enjoyed it' (1978: 14). As testimony to incest, '*Kiss Daddy Goodnight*' is lightly mocking, its significance skirts the surface of its meaning, it is not held by its presumed meaning, but this only belies considerable depth: in other words, we surely grasp the gravity of what is being said. When writing at her best, and certainly at the beginning, Armstrong does not freight language with the pathos of incest, of the pain caused to herself or others, but chooses instead a certain levity in telling the story of her incest experience and the experiences of those she spoke with; for the beauty of levity, as I understand it, is that it allows language to do more work for us by asking less of it. Language cannot carry the full weight of our political and personal desires, so better that we burden it with less expectation. We are going to have to unlearn what we think language can do for politics, if another story about the politics of giving testimony to violence is going to be told by feminists.

Acknowledgements

While I am grateful to everyone who has supported me during the development and writing of this book, I wish to take this opportunity to acknowledge those who have been particularly important in helping me through this process. First, then, I would like to thank my PhD supervisors Celia Lury and Jackie Stacey for their support during the writing of my thesis on which the book is based and while I accept all responsibility for the ideas here, I hope, nonetheless, it does some justice to their pedagogy.

Since finishing my PhD, I have had the pleasure of developing this book while working at the University of Salford and as a consequence I would like to thank the following three people. Elaine Baldwin, because I have enjoyed nothing more in the last six years than deferring to her on any matter I think of troubling her with. Antony Rowland, because it has been so easy to share ideas with him, which given the things we research and teach is something to be grateful for. And Graeme Gilloch, because whenever I needed encouragement I could always count on him to provide it in plenty.

Finishing and letting go of a long project is, however, the hardest point of writing and the point at which support is most needed. On this score, then, I am lucky to thank the following two people. Nicole Vitellone, because like any true friend, she provided unfailing support, especially in the last weeks of writing when I took up residence in her flat! And Mary Turner for caring as she did throughout the process – it made finishing a happy reality; I could not have asked for more.

And finally, I wish to thank my partner from whom I have learnt and come to know everything that is valuable in life, including the fact that if I heard *Dancing Queen* once, while writing this book, I heard it a hundred times as our children decided again and again to dance around the living room and thereby in my life. They are my joy.

With respect to copyright, I want to thank Linda Ness and Regina Lafay for giving me their permission to use their artwork and to note that Chapter Three was published in earlier form as 'A Withdrawn Vision: Art, Realism and the Scene of Incest' in the *Journal for Cultural Research*, vol. 8 (3): 217: 334; details of journal available at (http://tandf.co.uk/ journals).

Introduction: Undoing The Force of Violence

How can you know – in theory and in practice – what is an 'unbearable reality in fact' (Herman 1992: 102)? How do you remember a devastating experience if you have 'walled [it] off from conscious awareness and memory, so that it did not happen' (ibid.)? And how do you recover a history of violence when 'both the abuse and [the] coping strategies' are kept firmly 'outside of ordinary awareness' (ibid.: 103)? These are the types of question faced by Judith Herman when she argues in her critically acclaimed *Trauma and Recovery* that the 'ordinary response to atrocities is to banish them from consciousness' (ibid.: 1) and when she maintains that for victims of ongoing, inescapable abuse 'the ordinary relations of body and mind, reality and imagination, knowledge and memory no longer hold' (ibid.: 96). And they are questions faced by any clinician or critic, myself included, keen to figure the experience of violence as that which resists conscious recognition. For just how do you establish the impact of violence if it defies knowing or otherwise leaves a gap in understanding? How does trauma thereby alter our understanding of victim identity, consciousness and knowledge? And how do you secure the reality of a profound injustice if as a matter of routine it is not known as such or is forgotten? There are, of course, any number of ways of answering these questions, and how you answer them will depend on a number of key issues, including, for example, how or where you figure the source of critical agency; how you conceptualise memory and amnesia; and how you imagine the 'ordinary' relations of body and mind, reality and imagination, knowledge and memory to be in the first instance. And how you choose to answer them has analytical, cultural, political and social consequences.

This latter point is not lost on Herman. Indeed, *Trauma and Recovery* is fundamentally grounded in Herman's commitment to countering 'the denial of women's real experiences' of sexual and domestic violence (ibid.: 2), a project that she began before and with the 1981 publication of *Father–Daughter Incest*. Continuing in this vein *Trauma and Recovery* is dedicated to a politics of witnessing, 'truth-telling' and giving 'voice to the disempowered' (ibid.: 1, 9). Indeed, without a strong political movement to 'counteract the ordinary social processes of silencing and denial', Herman argues, 'the active process of bearing witness inevitably gives way to the active process of forgetting. Repression, dissociation, and denial are phenomena of social as well as individual consciousness' (ibid.: 9). *Trauma and Recovery* thus represents Herman's attempt to actively advance our understanding of violence and victimisation, and is thus meant to supplement our current understanding of post-traumatic stress disorder (PTSD). For while recognising the diagnostic importance of PTSD, Herman is, nonetheless, critical of its classificatory emphasis on events 'outside the range of human experience' since by definition certain victim experiences are left out. As she argues, 'Sadly, this definition has proved to be inaccurate. Rape, battery, and other forms of sexual and domestic violence are so common a part of women's lives that they can hardly be described as outside the range of ordinary experience' (ibid.: 33). As it currently stands, then, PTSD still does not 'fit accurately enough' the symptoms associated with the brutally quotidian experience of sexual and domestic violence, the latter of which is often far more complicated because the victim finds it difficult to escape (ibid.: 119).

In an effort to develop a typology that will do justice to the everyday, yet at times peculiar, victim reaction to sexual and domestic violence, Herman advances a notion of *complex* PTSD, a conceptual expansion of PTSD. Importantly, then, Herman is concerned with the ways in which victims who are held captive deny the knowledge of their experiences. In other words, she is interested in how and why victims of prolonged abuse actively forget what is happening to them. Distinguishing *Trauma and Recovery* from Herman's earlier work, and thus marking a particular shift in feminist and more general political thinking about victimisation, is, then, this emphasis on active forgetting and the implications held for victim testimony, a point stressed by Herman when she maintains that 'certain violations of the social compact are too terrible to utter aloud'; they are *'unspeakable'* (ibid.: 1). The emphasis on 'unspeakability' – and more broadly on 'unrepresentability' – is, then, the signal difference between this work and the work characterising early, radical feminist commentary on sexual violence, such as Armstrong's. Originally, victim silence was figured in terms of social censorship: women remained silent because there was a taboo on speaking about sexual violence, not because they had lost the capacity to talk per se. It was an externally imposed silence. This conceptualisation still holds for many, with victim silence still figuring as a consequence of social censorship manifest in any number forms, explicit and implicit. By drawing on her own rape experience, Cathy Winkler argues, for example, that silence is 'the choice of most victims' because they fear the consequences of reporting the rape to others or to the police (2002: 287). Indeed, for Winkler, the prospect of a negative social response censors women's desire to speak out because it is experienced like a 'rape', albeit a 'social rape' (ibid.). Thus she writes, 'Silence is a method of protection, protection from more rapes' (ibid.).

While acknowledging that silence is imposed externally, Roberta Culbertson also argues – by drawing from her own experience of childhood sexual abuse – that silence is 'an internal one in which the victim attempts to suppress what is recalled [. . .] or finds it repressed by some part of himself which functions as a stranger, hiding self from the self's experience according to unfathomable criteria and requirements' (1995: 169). More basically, she argues, internal silence represents the fact that the victim 'simply cannot make the leap to words' (ibid.). Importantly, then, Culbertson is complicating Winkler's vocabulary of choice, especially when, as Herman attests, the victim is a child and the violence a repetitive reality.

While in no way wishing to undermine the political significance of Winkler's reasoning, then, the aim of this book is to supplement feminist understanding of social censorship by stressing the psychological consequence of violence. In keeping with Herman, then, I am looking to develop a language that can sustain our understanding of victim experience precisely when securing recognition of that experience is a tenuous possibility, for, as Culbertson argues, when 'mind and body' conspire to 'deny in important ways the terror of the experience', the memories of violence are 'left apart from the story' (ibid.: 174).

How an emphasis on the psychic cost of violence plays out in theory and in politics is a point of major concern for this book, not least because for many commentators an emphasis on trauma is a neglecting of the question of social and political power. So, for example, in her article 'Toward a New Feminist Theory of Rape', Carine Mardorossian objects to 'making women's psyche the site of analysis' (2002: 756), since this 'reduces antirape politics to a psychic dimension' and as such it represents, for Mardorossian at least, a regressive moment in the history of feminist theory (ibid.: 747). According to Mardorossian this preoccupation with the personal and psychological dimensions of the rape experience simply repeats a long-standing, individualising and apolitical articulation of victimisation and interiority, which is to say a historically conservative desire to equate the workings of women's psyche with their victim status as opposed to an analysis of the social conditions of their lives.

Other critics have been even more scathing of 'the turn to trauma'. According to John Mowitt, for example, it represents an instance of a widespread tendency to displace the political with the ethical, where attempt is made to capitalise on the moral authority held by the appeal to pain and suffering. To this end, trauma theory repeats the moral logic of identity politics, and in so doing works within a framework established by liberal individualism, as critics of identity politics have always maintained and is certainly flagged by Armstrong as a logic of hierarchy and enumeration. Drawing inspiration from Wendy Brown's *States of Injury* (1995) and her claim that personal testimony politics is a project that cannot desire a future for itself because logically it cannot free itself from the past, Mowitt is unsettled by the failure of trauma theorists to reflect upon their common turf with liberalism, so that he maintains that 'if we are ever to find "the real killers," it will be because a movement has emerged that refuses to argue with the Right on its own terms' (2000: 284). For Mowitt, the popularity of trauma theory represents the continued failure of politics to secure an effective critique of liberalism and the conceits of individualism. Moreover, Mowitt argues, this turn to trauma is problematic because it obscures the 'work' done by politics: 'the labour of "making" sides, of producing and advancing positions' (2000: 294). Whereupon he argues that 'What is risked in this obscurity is not just the elaboration of the ethical as such (its production as "that which matters most"), but the importance of the political as the field within which groups struggle in and for power' (ibid.).

I share many of the concerns expressed by Mardorossian and Mowitt, hence the point of my book is to demonstrate how trauma theory can produce *political* understanding of violence and victimisation but without repeating the problems they flag up. This said, however, and as a summary riposte to Mowitt, it will by turn require a rethinking of what constitutes political labour and what constitutes the political field in which we work. Key to my aims is the writing of Cathy Caruth (1995, 1996) because as I understand her work she is looking to sever our understanding of trauma from liberal conceits; hence, as she argues, the 'attempt to gain access to a traumatic history' is a 'project of listening *beyond the pathology of individual suffering*, to the reality of a history that in its crises can only be perceived in unassimilable forms' (1995: 156, my emphasis). In other words, it is a project of *critical* reading and listening precisely because there is an attempt to get beyond privileging the individual as the site of trauma. However, what this means in practice is a point of intense theoretical and methodological debate, as I shall explore throughout this book. So while I agree with Mardorossian and many others besides when they insist that a language of trauma has tended to reproduce the possessive grammar of liberal individualism and the all too frequently pathological inferences of psychoanalysis and other psychotherapeutic languages (see, for example, Cvetkovich 2003), I also believe that via the work of trauma theorists such as Caruth, as well as Shoshana Felman and Dori Laub (1992), that it is now possible to separate our understanding of violence and victimisation from the precepts of liberal modernism and thereby meet Mardorossian's demand to retheorise 'the meanings of the categories such as "victim" and "experience" rather than merely criticize their use' (2002: 772).

Like Mardorossian, then, I am interested in retheorising the experience of sexual violence and thereby refiguring if not complicating political and especially feminist understanding of victimisation. But I depart quite considerably from Mardorossian in how I stage this process, since she is concerned with providing a 'contextual analysis of the ways in which experience is given meaning at a particular time and space' (ibid.: 747–8), whereas I am keen to argue that the force of violence is such that it radically disrupts how we might understand the parameters of time and space, and how once they are altered by violence they cannot be taken as points from which to infer meaning. What I wish to stress here is that the very idea of 'contextual' analysis and meaning is fundamentally altered by trauma not only because it is incomprehensible to the degree that it cannot be 'recalled in any way that admits of context and understanding; it simply has no narrative frame' (Culbertson 1995: 177), but also because, as Culbertson argues, the 'nonordinary reality' of violence has 'its own landscape, its own apparently metaphorical reality that is in fact not metaphorical at all' (ibid.: 188). Thus Culbertson speaks of how 'Trapped below [the everyday and the constructions of language], the violation seems to continue in a reverberating present that belies the supposed linearity of time and the possibility of endings' (ibid.: 170). In other words, time and space take on another reality for the traumatised victim of violence, and as a consequence determining its context and thereby its meaning is a complex task, to say the least.

A sense of this complexity can be glimpsed, for example, by considering the work of the feminist philosopher Susan J. Brison, who speculates on her rape experience in her book *Aftermath: Violence and the Remaking of a Self.* Written in the early 1990s and in the relative aftermath of the attack, Brison begins by arguing that rape requires 'the illumination provided by a victim's perspective' (2002: 4), even though she acknowledges that 'imagining what it is like to be a rape victim is no simple matter, since much of what a victim goes through is unimaginable. Still, it's essential to try to convey it' (ibid.: 5). In view of this caveat, and in reference to the events of 4 July 1990, Brison goes on to describe how she had been walking down a quiet, country lane in France when she was attacked from behind, strangled three times, raped and finally left for dead having had her skull smashed in. Commenting on her experience of the rape following the assailant's first attempt at strangulation and her subsequent loss of consciousness, she writes: 'When I awoke, I was being dragged by my feet down into the ravine. I had often, while dreaming, thought I was awake, but now I was awake and convinced I was having a nightmare. But it was no dream' (ibid.: 2). Although, ultimately, left in no doubt that something happened – a reality confirmed by her 'multiple head injuries', 'swollen shut' eyes and 'fractured trachea, which made breathing difficult' (ibid.: 2–3) – there is, nevertheless, a sense in which Brison finds the reality hard to grasp. It is this challenge that preoccupies Brison when she first sits down to write about the rape. Of this initial attempt, she writes:

> all I could come up with was a list of paradoxes. Things had stopped making sense. [. . .] I turned to philosophy for meaning and consolation and could find neither. Had my reasoning broken down? Or was it the breakdown of reason? I couldn't explain what had happened to me. [. . .] As a philosopher, I was used to taking something apparently obvious and familiar [. . .] and making it into something quite puzzling and strange. But now, when I was confronted with the utterly strange and paradoxical, philosophy was of no use in making me feel at home in the world. (ibid.: ix–x)

As Brison clearly testifies here, when reality and reason have parted company, there is no significance or comfort to be found in the rationalisations normally afforded by the habit(s) of knowledge, thus making a nonsense of the fact that she is a philosopher. Moreover, Brison argues that no amount of *prior* knowledge was able to prepare her for the reality of rape, for as she writes:

> Although I had been primed, since childhood, for the experience of rape, when I was grabbed from behind and thrown to the ground I initially had no idea what was happening. As I've mentioned earlier, I first experienced the assault as a highly unrealistic nightmare from which I tried to wake up. (ibid.: 88)

Knowing about rape in general does not prevent the reality being traumatic.

If Brison struggles with the reality as a known reality, this is partly because she 'didn't know the worst – the unimaginably painful aftermath of violence – was yet to come' (ibid.: x). She goes on to experience the impact of the rape in the days, weeks, months and years following the assault. Unable to shake off her experience, she also begins to learn that there is no limit to the trauma of rape: the idea that the rape took place on 4 July thus emerges as a convenient if not a punitive fiction given expectations of recovery, for, as Culbertson puts it, 'the memory of trauma, or the knowledge of things past' is dictated by a 'wild and skewed time' (1995: 176).

In a series of evocative scenes, Brison goes on to describe what it is like living the 'wild and skewed time' of trauma as she struggles to retain a sense of the present; so, for example, she describes how, when enduring a particularly long and insensitive examination by police surgeons (as if, she writes, they were performing an autopsy), she 'felt that [she] was experiencing things posthumously' (2002: 8). She continues:

> When the inconceivable happens, one starts to doubt even the most mundane, realistic perceptions. Perhaps I'm not really here, I thought, perhaps I did die in that ravine. The line between life and death, once so clear and sustaining, now seemed carelessly drawn and easily erased.
>
> For the first several months after my attack, I led a spectral exist-ence, not quite sure whether I had died and the world went on without me, or whether I was alive in a totally alien world. [...] I felt as though I'd somehow outlived myself. (ibid.: 8–9)

Haunted by a reality she struggles to assimilate, Brison is thus plagued by debilitating flashbacks and with them an inability to determine her own presence: is she here or there? Is she alive or is she dead? Does she haunt life or does death haunt her? Outliving violence changes one's grasp on reality precisely because it leaves one haunted by a death experience, an encounter with death that language cannot accommodate. 'For months after my assault,' Brison writes, 'I had to stop myself before saying (what seemed accurate at the time), "I was murdered in France last summer"' (ibid.: xi). She stops herself making this claim precisely because she knows that others will hear it only symbolically, when she imagines herself to be saying it literally. As Brison repeatedly testifies, 'I am not the same person who set off, singing, on that sunny Fourth of July in the French countryside. I left her in a rocky creek bed at the bottom of a ravine. I had to in order to survive' (ibid.: 21). Similarly, Culbertson is not being metaphorical when she maintains that the 'survivor survives twice: survives the violation; and survives the death that follows it' (1995: 191). Whatever testimony is, it is, as Caruth argues, 'The inextricability of the story of one's life from the story of a death, an impossible and necessary double telling' (Caruth 1996: 8).

The 'reality' of sexual violence is a spatially and temporally complex experience, and as such it complicates Mardorossian's ambition to think about rape as a concrete experience given meaning at a particular time and space. Indeed, Mardorossian's aspiration would already be undercut if she paused to consider the implications held by her observation that 'rape is a reality that feels anything but real to the victim' (2002: 765). Yet it is a critically radical statement, for it means that the objectively brute and overwhelming reality of rape can be read as subjectively *underwhelming*: indeed, *is* subjectively underwhelming; for as Mardorossian's statement implies, the experience of violence is not excessively and overpoweringly real – on the contrary, it does not feel especially real. Alternatively put: violence *is catastrophic because it does not register as a personal reality*. So while it might be thought that there is no experience more known, more our own, more personal than the experience of violence, the contrary is true: it is the experience least known, least our own and least personal, and as such, I want to argue, it remains permanently beyond our recuperating powers. Put conversely, it is the most abstract experience we are ever likely to mistakenly call our 'own', mistakenly because violence disrupts the possessive grammar of claiming any such experience as our own.

My position, here, can be clarified by reference to Culbertson. According to Culbertson violence produces the paradox 'of the distance of one's own experience' (1995: 170), yet she retains the possessive grammar of liberalism and the integrity of individuality, when subsequently arguing that 'no experience is more one's own than harm to one's own skin' (ibid.: 170), even if conceding that 'none is more locked within that skin, played out within it in actions other than words, in patterns of consciousness below the everyday and the constructions of language' (ibid.). Importantly for Culbertson, while the psyche might fail to register what is happening, the body remembers: deep down, below the surface of things, our bodies are keeping track of the violence. Of course, this is an appealing narrative but it only serves to entrench the possessive grammar of liberal individualism. To help clarify what I mean here (or why I find it troubling) I want to return to Herman, whose 'careful clinical account of the aftermath of violation' is acknow-ledged by Culbertson as being central to her own analysis' (ibid.: 193).

According to Herman the desire to deny the reality of violence is such that the victim is quite capable of forgetting what has hap-pened, and if not forgetting it, the victim is as likely to find the experience unspeakable, but, as I established, this poses a fun-damental problematic: for how do we guarantee the reality of vio-lence if, at best, it is no longer the reality you imagine and if at worst it disappears without a trace? How do you advance a cultural poli-tics of violence when the most violently defining moments of a life pass without leaving an impression? And how do you convey the unbearable reality of violence when its leaves you lost for words? It is at this point, however, that Herman's emphasis on trau-matic amnesia takes a qualifying turn when she quickly maintains that:

> Atrocities, however, refuse to be buried. Equally powerful as the desire to deny atrocities is the conviction that denial does not work. Folk wisdom is filled with ghosts who refuse to rest in their graves until their stories are told. Murder will out. (1992: 1)

Violence, according to Herman, will always announce its presence, its force being such that no matter how we might prefer to wish it away as a reality, it will return to haunt us. Thus she maintains that matching the 'will to deny horrible events' is a 'will to proclaim them aloud', the latter of which is driven by the reality of violence: by the very fact of its happening. Importantly, here, Herman works to per-sonify history by figuring 'atrocities' as 'ghosts' that are always speaking to us. So while she is ready to admit that violence alters the relations of 'body and mind, reality and imagination, knowledge and memory', these 'altered states of consciousness permit the elaboration of a prodigious array of symptoms, both somatic and psychological. And these symptoms simultaneously conceal and reveal their origins; they speak in a disguised language of secrets too terrible for words' (ibid.: 96). While we might try to bury it, truth will always seek or otherwise declare its presence. Try as we might and try with all our might, violence cannot be pushed permanently away as a secret: it will rise up. Therefore the impact of violence is understood by Herman – as well as Culbertson – with the potential to always reveal or show itself, especially if and when the social and psychic mechanisms designed to keep it at bay falter and wane. In an attempt to resolve the paradox violence is thereby formulated as that which can – if not always will – write its way back into consciousness (as conscious knowledge). Violence, you might say, is never lost on us.

The idea that violence is never lost to us, even though it is routinely forgotten, is absolutely compelling, and for many it stands as the merit of Herman's work: there is, it seems, no experience destined to be as real to us as violence, except perhaps sex as Culberston argues when she concludes her analysis. 'Terrible' as it might sound, Culbertson writes, but her 'secret' knowledge of violence is somehow 'compelling, if for no other reason that its firm rooting in the body, [. . .]. Like sex, it has a certain presence' (1995: 191) and as such the 'choice perhaps has to be made; self and identity versus intensity' (ibid.). But as I have argued above trauma does not necessarily manifest itself in this way: it can, indeed, fail to register with any such force; which I should stress is not the same as saying that the victim has grown numb to the experience of violence. But rather it is never grasped as real enough in the first instance to warrant a numbing response or reflex. Failing to register violence on this account is not, in other words, a form of wishful thinking as it is for Herman and in very different ways for a range of psychoanalytical thinkers, but evidence of the power of violence to leave us with nothing to show for its devastating impact; for as Shoshana Felman argues the *vanishing of the event* is part of 'its *actual historical occurrence*' (Felman and Laub 1992: 102). Contra Herman and Culberston, I am suggesting, then, that in some definitive sense violence is, indeed, lost on the victim.

As a feminist conceit, an emphasis on the *dissimulating reality of trauma* does not appear promising; indeed, as a political premise it risks a logic whereby women are structurally figured as having *nothing* meaningful to say. But as Judith Butler (2004b) has recently argued:

This is, of course, not to say that nothing is thought, that no story is told, and no representation made, but only to say that whatever story and representation emerge to account for this event, which is no event, will be subject to the same catachresis that I perform when I speak about it improperly as an event; it will be one that must be read for what it indicates, but cannot say, or for the unsayable in what is said. What remains crucial is a form of [political] reading that does not try to find the truth of what happened, but, rather, asks, what has this non-happening done to the question of truth? For part of the effect of that violation, when it is one, is precisely to make the knowing of truth into an infinitely remote prospect; this is its epistemic violence. To insist, then, on verifying the truth is precisely to miss the effect of the violation in question, which is to put the knowability of truth into enduring crisis. (ibid.: 156–7)

In a summary, but distinctly astute, fashion, Butler points up the political significance of trauma theory for feminism, for on the one hand, feminist critics will have to learn to read women's testimony to sexual violence according to different economy, one not predicated on the possibility of manifest meaning; and on the other hand, they will have to learn to fashion a politics not dependent on the possibility of establishing the truth of violence as something known. The aim of *Violence and The Cultural Politics of Trauma* is develop Butler's brief analysis which, following Caruth and the work of other trauma theorists, insists on a politics chastised by the limits to knowledge imposed by trauma – but not for that matter giving up on the questions of trauma, testimony and truth. Indeed, what emerges instead is a demand for a politics willing – and necessarily having – to speak 'improperly' about trauma and violence also, which to my mind will always have to be the case if we are to accept without equivocation that violence is 'an unbearable reality in fact'.

Chapter 1 is based for the first part on a reading of the recovered and false memory syndrome debates that raged through the 1990s and which arguably encapsulate the methodological challenges facing a contemporary politics of remembering and speaking out. Using a discussion of the response to the publication of Ellen Bass and Laura Davis's *The Courage to Heal* (1998), a phenomenally successful self-help book for women survivors of incest, I intend to show how the controversy caused by the book throws into relief the anxieties generated by an emphasis on radical amnesia and the implications held for thinking radically about the sociality of remembering. Turning away from the reaction provoked by this text in particular, the second part of this chapter deals more closely with the question of how we might read women's contemporary testimony by evaluating the post-structuralist reading offered by Donna J. Young, since at issue for me is how feminists might read testimonies without reducing them to statements on power. Indeed, given how trauma is understood to evade representation, the question of reading is for many trauma theorists the key question, for just how do you read that which escapes symbolic registration? The answer is that we learn to read for what is not and what cannot be said: namely we learn to listen to the silence left by violence. This might sound hopelessly conceited but, as I will argue with reference to the work of Kalí Tal, it is no more contrived than other strategies for reading trauma testimony, especially those relying on principles of contextualisation. In addition, I argue that by necessity the reading of trauma testimony must be imaginative, playful and to a certain extent irreverent. And while open to the charge of inappropriateness, I argue that the cogency of this charge is dependent on problematic assumptions about the autonomy of testimony and the role of language in politics.

Building on the methodological insights explored in the first chapter, the following chapters are based on the analysis of three key case-studies: a recovered memory autobiography, survivor art and a talk show, although I would stress that issues of analysis, interpretation and reading are never far from the surface. While not exhausting the popular archive of women's trauma testimony, they are nonetheless representative. Importantly, then, this book is based on testimony that is compromised by other institutional imperatives, hence as such they cannot carry political expectation in the manner demanded by early radical feminists. Thus they provide a clear test for how we might think through a cultural politics of trauma in the twenty-first century. But there are two additional reasons why this book is based on the reading of popular testimony. First, while trauma theory has been key to the writing of this book, it has been developed primarily in relation to canonical and perhaps more self-consciously literary testimony, notably Holocaust testimony. Therefore one of the challenges of this book was to test the value of trauma theory for a feminist politics of popular cultural testimony, which means in effect resisting the urge to hold up popular trauma testimony as equally rich in meaning. The test, in other words, was not to laud the qualities of popular cultural testimony, but try instead to stick to reading its perhaps cliched discourses. Second, as has been pointed out by Ann Cvetkovich in her book *An Archive of Feelings*, trauma itself raises questions about what 'counts as an archive' and thereby it raises questions about what 'counts as a public culture' (2003: 10). Cvetkovich uses her insight in order to argue that the affects associated with trauma also serve 'as the foundation for the formation of public cultures' (ibid.), whereas I would want to argue that the transitory nature of popular trauma testimony works, in fact, to add greater complexity to this problematic, thus a focus on the short life of popular testimony exemplifies the problems associated with archiving the trace of trauma. Third, and a related point, this book is based specifically on women's incest or child sexual abuse testimony, since it brings together a set of critical issues, including, for example, the question of the veracity of childhood traumatic memory, the political value of notions of innocence compared to the value of complicity, the voyeurism afforded by listening to sexually traumatic experiences and the limits of figuring sexual trauma as unrepresentable at a time when the gains made by radical feminism appear already to be slipping from us.

Chapter 2 is based on a reading of Sylvia Fraser's incest memoir *My Father's House*, a testimony written by her after forty years of amnesia. This chapter is key because while I suggested in the Preface that neither radical feminism nor feminist post-structuralism had theorised the experience of incest, psychoanalysis has, and has left a legacy of incredibly fraught debate. Built around the readings that have been made of *My Father's House*, this chapter offers a thorough exploration of the psychoanalytic debates of memory, fantasy and sexual abuse by tracking, in particular, the multiple meanings and use of repression. Critically I also interrogate how the conceptual move from reading the scene of incest based on a notion of hysteria towards a reading based on *Nachträglichkeit* alters the theoretical status of the event. This said, however, the chapter also attempts to push our theoretical language beyond the terms established by Jeffrey Masson in his *Assault on Truth* (1984), hence while I am keen to maintain a language of innocence I am also keen to alter how we might think about it.

Chapter 3 is based on the analysis of incest survivor art. The aim of this chapter is to push for a less redemptive reading of survivor art. Using readings of incest survivor art I explore the relationship of art, trauma and viewing subjectivity. In this chapter I position myself between the romanticism of someone like Alice Miller, for whom trauma always gives birth to creativity, and the cynicism of certain post-structuralist writers for whom popular trauma art is symptomatic of a morally simplistic discourse on violence and victimisation, as well as a simplistic view of representation as realist. In particular I advance a critique of their turn to conceptually based art, which in one way or another requires a logic of inspiration. Key then to this chapter is the idea that a politics of viewing incest art might look for a subject not inspired by what they see. Indeed, in this chapter I am keen to press for a logic of how little we get in return when viewing trauma art, how precious little we get to see. Thus I maintain we must counsel our desires to expect less: truth is not the picture of reality we expect and in the end we have learn to be poorer and not richer for 'knowing' when contemplating the translation of pain into paint.

Chapter 4 is twofold. Staged via Frigga Haug's feminist socialist reading of the global scene of child sexual abuse, the first part of this chapter looks to interrogate the possibility of speaking out in a profit-driven culture of confession. Via my discussion of Haug I argue that there is no place outside mass media culture, and if we are going to figure a future for a cultural politics of trauma, we have to think about how power works under the conditions of late modernity. This said, however, I express doubt whether Haug's recourse to precepts of socialist feminism are adequate to the task and I express a concern over her dismissive reading of women speaking out about personal traumas. Turning to a discussion of a British daytime talk-show – *Kilroy* – dedicated to women speaking about their experiences of sexual abuse, I explore how we might reconfigure the political significance of their testimony. Key to my efforts is an emphasis on the serial, nebulous and essentially impersonal nature of such testimony, and how it might be related to our understanding of graffiti.

CHAPTER 1

It's All in the Reading: Moving Beyond the False Memory Syndrome Debates

In her recent book *Relational Remembering: Rethinking the Memory Wars*, Sue Campbell provides an incredibly sustained feminist philosophical interrogation of the controversy caused by the phenomenon of so-called 'false memory syndrome', the appellation given by a lobbying group of apparently wrongly accused parents to describe how and why their daughters 'remember' abuse in therapy when, it is claimed by the parents, nothing of the sort has occurred, and in so doing she explores the implications for our understanding of the sociality of memory. Needless to say, the debates generated by the charge that therapists are responsible for 'suggesting' to their clients that they have forgotten a history of abuse – which the clients subsequently take as read – have taxed feminist thinking, most of which struggles in one way or another with the question of memory's autonomy. Typically, then, it is asked: is memory uniquely our own? Does 'our' memory depend on others and other outside resources? How can you remember something that did not happen to you? Can you? Are victims of violence more or less likely to recall their own history? Can others recall it for you? And finally, given the phenomenal explosion of recovered memory therapy and apparent proliferation of incest memories is there not reason to be sceptical?

Inevitably, feminist opinion differs and is itself frequently split on these questions, with feminists struggling in particular with a desire to uphold the authority and integrity of women's memory and testimony to child sexual abuse when there appears to be ground for doubt. Self-questioning has become the order of the day: as Campbell argues, feminist critics are expressing 'caution about certain types of therapy and the dangers of suggestion and overt influence', and certainly almost all critics 'acknowledge the possibility of a client's developing illusory memories to confirm a therapist's hypothesis about the origins of the client's difficulties' (2003: 14). As Campbell correctly asserts, feminists have not been naive or unquestioning in their response to the charge of 'false memories'. So, here is the rub, for as keen as feminists might be to deny the possibility of 'false memories', the phenomenon exists as a 'complicated possibility' for a whole host of cultural, political and social reasons (Bowman and Mertz, cited by Campbell 2003: 7). Not least among these is that recovered memory therapists, including Judith Herman – whom Campbell spends a chapter discussing – but most particularly Ellen Bass and Laura Davis, authors of the phenomenally successful self-help book *The Courage to Heal*, insist on their faith that repression and dissociation are a reality, and while there might be very little concrete evidence to suggest a history of abuse, this alone does not mean that nothing has happened. Quite the contrary. It just means that there is little sign or pretext for reading (if ultimately 'nothing' to decipher). If false memories are a complicated possibility, then a belief in repressed memory is a prime complicating reason, if not the prime complication.

This point is not lost on Louise Armstrong, whom I discussed in the Preface. Armstrong, as I argued, has long been troubled by the power of psychotherapeutic discourse and is clearly vexed by the prospect that 'We have become a population of stories that carry no larger meaning, that imply no social issue, but are the wampum, the currency, that is the trade of the incest survivor identity' (1994: 38). But this concern is nothing if held against the possibility that women are now being 'encouraged' to remember events that might be nothing more than the confabulated currency of therapy. Thus Armstrong recalls an *Oprah Winfrey* show dedicated to women 'who claimed that they had been brainwashed into believing that they had been sexually abused as children – and were now certain they had not' (ibid.: 5). On the panel, Armstrong recalls, was Bass, who alongside Armstrong was among the first radical feminists concerned with breaking the silence when she co-edited the 1983 incest testimony anthology *I Never Told Anyone*, but who is now (only) known as the co-author of *The Courage to Heal*. Bass was on the show, as Armstrong notes, 'supporting the endorsement of survivor veracity',

'Surely an excellent and necessary thing to do', Armstrong comments (ibid.). 'But' as Armstrong continues, 'here is the catch':

> No matter how much one implicitly trusts that suppressed memories do emerge in adulthood, the charge used by those challenging the reality of claimed assault is correct: the book does not require real memory, offering instead the assurance that if you think you were abused, if you feel you might have been abused, you probably were. Within this loose construction lurks the invitation to turn some dreadful actuality of paternal child rape into an experiential metaphor. (ibid.: 5)

Although not dismissing the possibility that memories of abuse can be suppressed – which is to say consciously forgotten – Armstrong is, nonetheless, voicing profound reservations about the possibility of a radical amnesia, and in this sense she shares an anxiety with many others over the plausibility of repressed memory and the role of therapists in eliciting memory when credence is given to the possibility of complete forgetting. Indeed, for Armstrong this 'loose construction' is illustrative of exactly how, as she puts it, 'twisted' the politics of remembering sexual abuse has become, with psychotherapeutic discourse imagined here, by Armstrong at least, not only with the power to send women out into the world with words empty of (political) meaning but more radically with the power to send women out into the world with memories empty of reality, memories without a proper stake in reality. Following Armstrong's line of thinking, the problem is not that self-help literature simply places an individualist emphasis on helping yourself to cope with the reality of sexual abuse such that it is politically meaningless as a project for radical change, but that it is also figured by Armstrong as quite literally encouraging a 'help yourself' (to the memory of others) mentality. In other words, 'real' victims are at risk of losing their patent claim on reality; 'real' memory, it seems, is up for grabs.

Leaving aside for the moment Armstrong's own scepticism, the challenges posed by the commitment to radical amnesia such that it 'allows' women to claim a history of abuse with something as vague as a thought or as nebulous as a feeling raises another set of critical questions for feminists, if less frequently asked: is radically uncertain memory or unconnected feeling enough for politics, and if so how do we read it and the testimony it engenders? What if violence leaves us no sign at all? How, then, do we read its memory? How do we analyse a history of abuse if it returns as (less than) nothing, with little or no evidence to suggest itself? Or when the victim has little or nothing to say on the matter? These are the questions that I am keen to pursue in this chapter for, as I noted in the Introduction, perhaps the most important consequences of an emphasis on the unrepresentability of trauma are the implications held for reading, for whatever the answer to these questions, it is most likely as, Thomas Elsaesser argues, that we will have to 'suspend the normal categories of [political] story-telling' and 'revise our traditional accounts of narrative and narration' (2001: 199). In other words, we will have to use a little imagination.

Demanding that we employ our imagination is, of course, easier said in theory, than done in practice, for, as Campbell argues, 'many feminists have felt constrained in their responses to these controversies by their own concerns about the manipulation of women by experts and the vulnerability of memory to distortion through reconstruction' (2003: 7). Indeed, Campbell expresses a deep concern that the debates sprung by the charge of false memory syndrome will inevitably direct how we think about the relational aspects of remembering. This is a really key point. As Campbell argues,

> The harmful stereotypes of women's passivity that have repopulated discussions of abuse have led many theorists to regard the social dimensions of remembering only negatively, as a kind of threat or contaminant to memory; they have led them to restrict an analysis of power relationships to a discussion of how authority figures like therapists can exercise a damaging influence over our views of the past. (ibid.: 8)

'But', Campbell contends, 'a discussion of the relational dimensions of remembering primarily in terms of the threat of memory distortion compromises our understanding of the sociability of memory' (ibid.). Memory, as Campbell so rightly argues, is always already social; it always requires the presence of others, which is why False Memory Syndrome Foundation (FMSF) rhetoric is so deeply problematic and why we should resist any pressure to rein in our political imagination.

Significantly, then, Campbell argues that the controversy over the false memory debates serves as 'an excellent opportunity to think about some of the relational dimensions to memory experience, memory competencies, and memory narratives' (ibid.: 8). Importantly, though, for Campbell and in an attempt to clear the necessary space for thinking through these issues, this does not mean seeking 'a conciliatory "middle," or common, ground' (ibid.: 13). Indeed, she is adamant that the call for a middle ground is a way of distancing knowledge production from politics by figuring, hence disavowing, some positions on memory as 'extreme', most notably those associated with an explicit politics. Thus Campbell argues that 'the call for a middle ground' makes 'it very difficult to respond adequately to the politics of these controversies' (ibid.: 13–14).

I could not agree more with Campbell on the question of the 'middle ground', as she has formulated it, since adopting so-called common ground cannot but work to concede power when this might not be your express aim. So, for example, I do not think for a minute that Armstrong wants to yield any ground to FMSF lobbyists, but when she looks to distance herself from Bass and Davis, and seek some perhaps safer ground for a politics of sexual abuse memory, she finds herself, unwittingly, sharing some conservative if not reactionary ground, as I shall demonstrate.

While Armstrong is more or less silent on the political dilemmas and theoretical issues raised by *The Courage to Heal*, thus leaving readers to draw their own conclusions, other commentators have not been so quiet or retiring in their conclusions. Indeed, if any single one thing caused the memory wars to explode as they did, it was the popular success of *The Courage to Heal*. There is no other text that has figured so prominently in the FMSF rhetoric or has been so key to those wishing to critique the recovered memory movement. So, for example, the 1995 text *The Memory Wars*, written by a distinctly vociferous critic of the recovered memory movement, Frederick Crews, can easily be seen as the rhetorical counterpart of *The Courage to Heal*. Originally published as two articles for *The New York Review of Books*, Crews's book is a barely contained critique of Freud and the recovered memory movement. Although to the extent to which 'the relatively patent and vulgar pseudoscience of recovered memory rests in appreciable measure in the respectable and entrenched pseudoscience of psychoanalysis', it is 'the perniciousness of the recovered memory movement' that bears the brunt of his critical attack, because psychoanalysis did not have the power to wreak social harm until it fell into the 'coarser hands' of Bass and Davis, since it was at this point that 'a countless number of deluded people (mostly women) were encouraged into launching false charges of sexual abuse against their dumbfounded and mortified elders' (1995: 4–5).

Key to his critical take on repression and its mobilisation by the recovered memory movement is the part played by the therapist in the production of memories. Quite simply, for Crews, there is a 'blindness to the role of therapy itself in producing behaviour that gets mistaken for the residue of long-buried trauma from the patient's early years', which itself is an error that 'partakes of a much wider insensitivity to suggestion – a shortcoming whose roots can be found in Freud's stubborn faith, in defiance of explicit challenges on the point, that messages from the unconscious are by and large incorruptible' (ibid.: 14). Indeed, here the recovered memory movement which is characterised by Crews as the 'stepchild' of psychoanalysis appears to be repeating the ignorance, if not sins, of the father. In sum, then, the central liability of the recovered memory movement is, according to Crews, that 'the therapist's presupposition that childhood sexual abuse is the likeliest cause of adult misery' does, indeed, 'issue in specious "memories" on the suggestible patient's part' (ibid.: 14). Or more succinctly, as he puts it later: 'where repression was, there shall suggestion be' (ibid.: 181).

Driving Crews's desire to critique the recovered memory movement and the idea of robust repression is how easily it allows for a rewriting of family history. Crews simply does not credit with any plausibility the idea that history can suddenly and mysteriously appear from no where. For him, historical consciousness is or must work as a progressive, steady accreditation of knowledge such that it can be (easily) tracked; it is not something that appears in and of our instant making, whereby it is unavailable for empirical testing and verification. History cannot come into being as if by magic, or at least if it does it must appear at the behest of a powerful instigator. Accordingly Crews writes that psychoanalysis and the recovered memory movement 'stand closer to animistic shamanism than to science', and it 'must be discarded if, once and for all, we are to bring psychotherapy into safe alignment with what is actually known about the mind' (ibid.: 29), which for Crews can be tantamount only to that which is actually known *by* the mind. Quite clearly Crews is haunted both by the unscientific nature of repression and the licence it gives for conjuring any manner of belief (or maybe more accurately the licence it gives women for revising family history). Indeed, he returns time and time again to the fact that repression cannot be scientifically proven, hence inducing popular belief in the theory of repression must by necessity become a literary or textual affair. He writes:

> The very idea of repression and its unraveling is an embryonic romance about a hidden mystery, an arduous journey, and a gratifying neat denouement that can ascribe our otherwise drab shortcomings and pains to deep necessity. When that romance is fleshed out by a gifted storyteller who also bears impressive credentials as an expert of the mind, most readers in our culture will be disinclined to put up intellectual resistance. (ibid.: 166)

Bass and Davis, do not figure, in this instance, as his object of critique, but Crews does cite Lenore Terr as a 'fluent ally' of the recovered memory movement and as the author of the highly influential and 'deftly written book' *Unchained Memories: True Stories of Traumatic Memories Lost and Found*. In a commentary that passes over his question as to whether 'Terr [isn't] simply handing herself a conceptual blank check' (when Terr maintains that trauma is a unique historical experience that rewrites the rules of memory), Crews concludes in dismay that 'If Terr is right about the special character of real-world trauma, we may have to fall back on sheer stories after all' (ibid.: 167). This emphasis on the power of storytellers and storytelling is central to Crews's theory of how suggestion works, since for him it is the 'seductive' and 'romantic' nature of trauma stories that is understood by him to be recruiting a wider female reading public; hence he writes, 'Just such solicitation – we can think of it as suggestion-at-a-distance – has by now been brought to bear on myriad vulnerable people, mostly women, by advocates in search of ideological and/or financial gain' (ibid.: 189).

It is at this point in his argument that Crews brings the full weight of his critique to bear on *The Courage to Heal*, since he considers Bass and Davis to be 'the most successful communicators' of the reality of repression, describing them respectively as 'a teacher of creative writing and her student' and as 'radical feminists who lacked any background in psychology' (ibid.: 192), but who through 'the icy formalism inculcated' by their 'recovery manual' (ibid.: 204) have ensured that recovery is 'not about surmounting one's tragic girl-hood but about keeping the psychic wounds open, refusing forgive-ness or reconciliation, and joining the permanently embittered corps of "survivors"' (ibid.: 194). Critiquing 'Bass and Davis's model of extracting repressed truths from the unconscious like so many bills from an automatic teller' (ibid.: 215), Crews concludes that these 'young fanatics' and 'romanticists' will eventually be defeated, because 'once the bizarre and sinister features of the recovered memory movement are widely known, sophisticated readers will not hesitate to distance themselves from it' (ibid.: 206).

There is, of course, plenty to say about Crews's commentary, but suffice it to say that by suggesting, as I have done, some common ground between Armstrong and Crews, I am not looking to demon-strate the naivety of Armstrong; indeed given how quiet Armstrong is on the matter and given how critical she normally is of psy-chotherapy, she has obviously chosen wisely to keep her counsel. But rather my point is that when Armstrong formulates her understand-ing of politics in terms of 'real memory', she is sharing some very fraught ground, ground which for Crews at least is governed by – and thereby restricted to – what can be known by the mind and measured by science. This I would argue is not the grounds on which to build a feminist politics of sexual abuse memory, for feminists have long since argued that science is not a natural ally, but more importantly, as Judith Butler argues, trauma 'takes its toll on empiricism' (2004b: 154). Thus I am keen to follow Campbell in her desire not to concede ground to the FMSF lobbyists such as Crews, and I am also keen to follow her when she argues that we must take the debates as an oppor-tunity to launch our own critical investigations into the sociality of memory, an opportunity clearly missed by Armstrong. This said, however, it is also, I would argue, an opportunity missed by

Campbell. Since in her desire to distance herself from the position held by Bass and Davis – Campbell makes only one reference to *The Courage to Heal* and this is buried in a footnote (which given the fact that her book is dedicated to the controversy sparked in no small measure by *The Courage to Heal* is a striking omission) – she fails to grasp the challenge presented by trauma: namely its resistance to any project of understanding. For as Cathy Caruth argues, the debates concerning false memories 'suggest that the problem of what it means to remember traumatic experience and what it means to know or recognise trauma in others is defined, in part, by the very way that it pushes memory away' (1995: viii). In some way absolutely funda-mental to the experience, then, trauma refuses to make itself known to anyone.

Following Caruth, then, it is possible to argue that the reality of traumatic memory and the role played by others in its production are not easily grasped, and by turn this means, as Caruth writes, when following the insights of Terr in a different direction to Crews: 'there may not be one simple, generalisable set of rules that can determine in advance the truth of any particular case, and we may thus ulti-mately have to struggle with the particularity of each individual story in order to learn anew, each time, what it means for a memory to be true' (1995: viii-ix). This is a distinctly radical commitment but it is a possibility Campbell rejects when she asserts, for example, that 'the question of whether people can recover memories of childhood sexual abuse or whether they sometimes seem to remember abuse that didn't happen' is 'beyond reasonable doubt' and therefore 'the real issues are elsewhere' (ibid.: 14). I do not share Campbell's con-fidence or conclusion, here. But rather in keeping with Caruth, I would suggest that the question of whether people can recover memories of childhood sexual abuse is a question not easily answered by what can count as 'reasonably' known, especially if Terr is right to stress that trauma rewrites the laws of memory. Indeed despite her claims to be rejecting designated positions, Campbell's commitment to the importance of philosophy suggests, I would hazard, a distrust of story-telling, which while not necessarily putting her on same ground as Crews, suggests that her under-standing of sociality might be restricted to less than radical ground. Indeed, how else are we meant to make sense of a model of *relational* memory when Campbell argues that 'we are not there, even as imaginary interlocutors, to question or press the client about her account of the past' (ibid.: 77). To what extent is her emphasis on relationality an actual rethink, if the memory of others is held as a separate account beyond challenge? How does Campbell's emphasis on the sociality of memory compare, for example, to Shoshana Felman's claim that 'The Other is necessary [. . .] for the history of trauma, to be written, to be constituted at all' (Felman 2002: 175, fn.3). And how does it compare to Dori Laub's claim that 'The emergence of the narrative which is being listened to – and heard – is, therefore, the process and the place wherein the cognizance, the "knowing" of the event is given birth to. The listener, therefore, is a party to the creation of knowledge *de novo*', and that the 'testimony to the trauma thus includes its hearer, who is, so to speak, the blank screen on which the event comes to be inscribed for the first time' (Felman and Lanb 1992: 57). And finally how does it compare to Caruth's claim that the history of a trauma 'can only take place through the listening of another' (1995: 11). The aim of the rest chapter is to explore these questions with a view to arguing that the emphasis placed on the role of the other by Felman, Laub and Caruth demands an infinitely more radical rethink of the sociality of memory than that suggested by Campbell, and in so doing it will require us to radically rethink the importance of language, storytelling and our methods thereby for reading women's testimony.

At this point I want to turn Donna J. Young's 'Remembering Trouble: Three Lives, Three Stories', an analysis of the narratives of three generations of women living in rural New Brunswick, Canada, since she begins her analysis with express reference to the work of Felman and Laub (though the essay appears in the distinctly Foucault-inspired *Tense Past: Cultural Essays in Trauma and Memory*, ed, Antze and Lambek, 1996). Based on ethnographic field work, Young's analysis of the women's stories of abuse and violence is an insightful account of the power of discourses in shaping the ways in which we remember, and she clearly illustrates how the discursive fields of the women – who are identified as Grandmother, Mother and Daughter (who is also acknowledged as a personal friend and as her point of entry into the remote community) – are historically and socially determining. As a consequence, Young demonstrates how their acts of remembering are respectively shaped by the religious rhetoric of the earlier part of the century, the consumer culture of the 1950s and 1960s and the contemporary medical language of psychiatry, especially the therapeutic discourses of recovered memory, post-traumatic repression and dissociation.

From the outset, however, Young is mindful of the limits of analysing 'discourse', warning, for example, of the poverty of '[h]astily drawn abstractions [when] charting a dominant discourse at a particular moment' (1996: 41). As a consequence, Young is careful to reflect on her approach by noting that

> what is at stake in collecting life stories is not a simple reconstruction of the empirical historical past, nor an indulgent and by turns condescending exploration of another's subjective, and therefore flawed, understanding of events that have passed, 'but the very historicity of the event in an entirely new dimension'. (Young 1996: 25, citing Felman and Laub 1992: 62)

Importantly, Young is sensitive to the fact that reading testimony is not about providing a simple record of events, nor a using of testimony as a pretext for demonstrating its limits, but rather of establishing the actuality of the events of which people speak in an 'entirely new dimension'. In other words, Young is conscious of the power of the interpreter and the ways in which the historicity of events – the very fact that they have happened – can be lost in the thick of reporting on the reality or else analysing its discursive production. By invoking the work of Felman and Laub, Young is clearly acknowledging a concern with the women's actual experiences of violence: the 'real' of their experiences.

Following Felman and Laub, Young thus endeavours to make an analytical space for the reality of trauma by acknowledging that 'there is a creative and formative tension between the ways in which stories are embedded in historical, political, economic, and ideological worlds *and the ways in which narratives create those worlds*' (ibid.: 25, my emphasis). By emphasising this tension between the context and testimony, Young seeks to ameliorate the ways in which an emphasis on the constitutive function of a discourse can result in crude, almost positivistic determinism (and thereby become little more than ideological critique). This is an important recognition on the part of Young, especially when she analyses how the 'psychoanalytic discourse of repression and dissociation' work to shape Daughter's memories as they emerge in therapy, for certainly the FMSF lobbyists admit no such subtlety. So although Young is clearly critical of how 'the literality of the therapist's interpretation of [Daughter's] nightmares and memory flashes denies, and so erases, the historical and cultural context within which Daughter's imagination and language unfurled' (ibid.: 38), Young's express aim is to restore a sense of that context, but doing so, as I have noted, without losing sight of Daughter's testimony. Thus she writes of how 'embedded in her story of once repressed and now recovered memories are the remnants of a childhood situated at the crossroads of changing, and utterly incommensurable, cosmologies' (ibid.: 26).

Despite this overt sensitivity – which is reiterated when Young insists that 'this exploration of family history over three generations assumes a dialectic tension between *context* and *text*' (ibid.: 26) – her commitment to maintaining a sense of the text is soon lost in practice. In spite of theoretical allusions to the textuality of the context, which is to insist on the irreducibility of history and life stories to context at the very least, Young, nevertheless, maintains that the anecdotal fragments she has chosen 'act as a "diagnostic of power" . . . revealing as they do, "historical shifts in configurations or methods of power"' (ibid.: 26, citing Abu-Lugkod). Thus she reads the life stories of the women as a diagnosis 'of both the ideological and discursive shifts that engender new constructions of narrative identity within new moral orders' (ibid.: 25). In spite of positing a less than given relationship between a text and 'its' context, Young proceeds here as if there were an ostensibly straightforward relationship between them, which is confirmed when she writes that 'transformations of power are *mirrored* in the very forms of textual disclosure and language within which the women couch their tales' (ibid.: 26, my emphasis). It seems, then, that Young has no trouble in reading the women's narratives. They are, in the final analysis, strangely transparent as Young reads them, quite literally, as stories revealing the 'truth' of the power of discourse. So, for example, Young maintains that Daughter's 'therapists, and countless books on childhood and ritual abuse written for a public with an enormous appetite for salacious stories, *convinced* her that within her recovered memories, her Self, lay a horrible truth' (ibid.: 42, my emphasis). 'But will this story be hers?' Young asks. The simple answer for Young is no.

I cannot stress enough that Young's analysis is insightful and as such it is a rich piece of discourse analysis. However, on this count, it is not an example of the type of reading pushed for by Felman and Laub. They mean something other than using testimony as a diagnostic of power, for as they argue when stressing the importance of reading text and context in conjunction – a strategy of analysis they call 'shuttle reading' – it is not a question of returning to the purely academic "mirror-games" between the "novel" and "life" and to the traditional, all-too-familiar critical accounts of the mutual "reflection" (or "representation") between "history" and "text"' (Felman and Laub 1992: xiv–xv).

> But is rather, and more challengingly, so as to attempt to see – in an altogether different and exploratory light – how issues of biography and history are neither simply represented nor simply reflected, but are reinscribed, translated, radically rethought and fundamentally worked over by the text. In order to gain insight into the significance and impact of the context on the text, the empirical context needs not just to be *known*, but to be *read*; to be read in conjunction with, and as part of, the reading of the text. (ibid.)

This summary exposition is already enough to show the limits of Young's understanding. It is not a question of mirroring, but rather a question of exploring how testimony alters our conceptualisation of 'its' context and how it might – or might not – be known. At issue for Felman and Laub, and the reason why they query what constitutes the context of testimony, is a concern over when and where testimony gets written in the first place. For as I noted above, Felman and Laub stress that testimony is only ever written or else constituted at the point of reception, in the presence of another. There is no historical record prior to this moment, no context as such. So when, for example, Laub argues that 'the "knowing" of the event is given birth to' at the point of reception, he means that testimony and any significance it has as a testimony is given to us only in the moment of listening and reading. There is no idea of memory before memory. It is not, then, a case of holding the language of survivors up to the light to catch a glimpse of how it is shot through with the meaning culled from cultural discourses as Young maintains, but rather it is a case of looking to create language in the light of the moment.

When Young reads the 'fragmented story' of Daughter – which is taken by Young to represent Daughter's attempt 'to recover/ re-create a life history in the wake of post-traumatic memory loss' – none of this understanding of how testimony is given can be found in her reading. So although Daughter is her point of entry into the research, and even though Daughter 'with considerable skill' sabotages Young's 'best-laid plans' as she 'go[es] out in search for clues that would unravel the significance of her night terrors' (1996: 35), and even though Young 'had the sense that [she] was travelling away from [her] project (at that point still firmly rooted in the prosaic) to probe the mysteries of the otherworldly, a task better suited to spirit mediums than to anthropologists' (ibid.: 34), and even though it became obvious to Young that her 'role was to serve as a bridge between the two worlds her life uncomfortably straddles' (ibid.: 35), she does not allow any of this disruption or tension to reconfigure the parameters of her reading. Daughter's testimony is read more simply as a statement on power, not as a potential statement on trauma. This lack of attention to the question of reading trauma narratives is most evident when Young analyses the journals written by Daughter for her therapists, which again are another example of the Daughter's disruptive influence, since she refuses to be interviewed by Young, protesting instead that she had already written her life story for her therapists, thereby insisting on giving her therapy journals to Young.

Basing her analysis on these journals, Young begins, however, by arguing that 'over the course of therapy the journal entries shift radically from the world in which Daughter presently struggles to one previously repressed', whereupon 'previously repressed memories are incorporated as facts into the reports (ibid.: 36). As the stress on repressed memories becoming facts clearly suggests, Young reads the changing concerns and language of the journal entries as a sign of the encroaching power of a discourse preoccupied with the past as a secret, undiscovered reality. Thus the differences between the two excerpts (one drawn from spring 1991 and one from spring 1992) are offered as indicators of Daughter's enculturation and her production as a subject 'driven to uncover the motley facts of her case history' (ibid.: 42). The first excerpt is understood as testament to Daughter's relative freedom from dominant trauma discourses, since it is written with an informal, lay understanding of her experiences. The second excerpt is read, however, as a sign of the saturating power of therapeutic discourses, which is evidenced, according to Young, by a distinct alteration in tone and content. The second extract reads:

> I researched all kind of books and articles on neuroscience, particularly night-terrors, eye-sight and hallucinations. I discovered that what I experience are hypnagogic hallucinations. It makes sense to me now . . . It is my understanding that an area in the occipital lobes (visual cortex) takes signals received from the eyes and 'forms' what we see, then sends those images to our consciousness (thought, recognition, and acknowledgement) to be acknowledged. So it seems to me that what happens when you have hypnagogic hallucinations is that the occipital lobes must be picking up visual signals from elsewhere. I think that the occipital lobes are getting signals from the temporal lobes where memories are stored. In memory loss or blocking out, the memories have not disappeared, it is the *accessing* of memories which has stopped. (Daughter cited in Young 1996: 37)

Using the content of this second piece of writing and its expressive difference from the first as the basis for her analysis, Young is quick to discredit Daughter's testimony by arguing that Daughter's technical competency represents her seduction by the language of psychiatry and thus her own thwarted desire to become an expert. Young writes:

> Placed within the context of Daughter's frustrated ambitions to be a scientist, I find the tenor of these excerpts sadly revealing. Daughter splits before our very eyes: one Self, would-be medical researcher, detached and objective, offering for dissection her other Self as patient. Denied entry into the world of the educated middle class as an equal, Daughter trades her ravaged psyche as currency for acceptance into a class to which she aspires. (ibid.: 37)

Leaving aside the fact that the second excerpt was written as formal letter by Daughter to an expert in the field and not as an informal journal entry (which would account, in part, for the shifting style and substance), what is troubling about Young's analytical privileging of discourse is her failure to engage with Daughter's testimony to traumatic experiences. I will stress, again, that I do not wish to deny that Daughter's language is difficult and requires interrogation or, indeed, to simply chide Young for voicing her concerns about the validity of Daughter's account. But rather I wish to assert that Daughter can be read as saying something other than what is dictated by dominant discourse.

Again while I have no objection to Young's doubling of commentary whereby she substitutes her reading of Daughter's journals for the therapists' presumed reading, I do object to her failure to read beyond the terms of her critique. For despite Daughter's expressed dislike of the analogy of splitting (Daughter writes: 'I do think "splitting" is a major form of coping. We all split in varying degrees. But I don't like the analogy of being two different people', ibid.), Young promptly invokes it. Young's failure to read continues, moreover, when she speculates on the success of Daughter's 'attempt' to write her past. Here Young's commentary is singularly dismissive, when she writes:

> What I find sad about my friend's attempt to write her life is how abysmally it fails. Rarely does she describe an event by placing herself squarely in the action of the unfolding story. One almost wonders if she was ever there at all. (ibid.)

But is it not possible to read Daughter's account as precisely to struggle the write about one's 'own' trauma? So when Young reads Daughter's inability to 'construct a life story' and inability to 'wrest her story away from her interlocutors [by whom I guessing that Young means her therapists]' as evidence of the grip of power, might it not be read as evidence of her struggle to get a grip on trauma and how she would, indeed, have no story to tell without her interlocutors? And when Young argues that Daughter's voice has become 'the voice of an outsider, or, perhaps more to the point, a would-be outsider' (ibid.), might we not read this as a struggle to speak about something on which you do not have the inside track?

I should add here that I am not trying to trump Young's reading with the 'truth' of my own. But rather I am trying to suggest that we might try to find ways of reading that do justice to the trauma suffered. Because despite her critical commentary, Young is in no doubt that Daughter suffered distinct trauma. As Young clearly details, Daughter was molested by her neighbour; lost her memory at the age of ten, when she and her siblings spent a winter alone with their father following desertion by the mother; lost her brother in a tragic accident and her other brother when he was forced to leave the family home by a brutal stepfather; and finally, as Young acknowledges, throughout her teenage years 'Daughter spent most of her energy avoiding the sexual advances of the [stepfather]' (1996: 40). Given all this it is hardly surprising that Daughter finds it difficult to write a story at which she is at the centre, since this is to ask her to write the story of a life which by description, here, is enough to push anyone to the limits of what they can reasonably grasp as their 'own'. Daughter's life was not in her possession and so she was, indeed, removed from the most significant events of her life. If the reference to a traumatic experience is taken as our guide (rather than an analytical concern with discourse), or indeed if we strive to read testimony in the context or field of trauma, it is possible to argue that Daughter's attempt to write her life does not read solely according to the strictures of discourse, but registers, if Young is right in diagnosing a haunting failure, the limits of all and any recovery. Her account fails to secure credibility precisely because her experiences of traumatic abuse are beyond even her own handling. In a very real sense, Daughter does not own her story, and to this end Young is right but for the wrong reasons. Daughter's story does not belong to her because it resists the language in which it might be told: words cannot do it justice. So when Young concludes that while she might have a greater historical knowledge of the settlement in which the women lived out their lives, yet might have failed 'to understand the local character of human existence at particular points in history' (ibid.: 42), she is not wrong, but nor is she wrong in her desire to offer the insight to Daughter, since it requires a degree of understanding neither of them has at their disposal, for as Geoffrey Hartman argues, 'The real – the empirical or historical origin – cannot be known as such because it presents always within the resonances or field of the "traumatic"' (1995: 543–4).

If Daughter's 'fragmented story' – which is beyond doubt a testimony to unknown loss – is going to be read as a trauma text, it will require feminists to read very differently, for, as Hartman argues, the story of trauma is 'a statement of a different sort', one which 'relates to the negative moment in experience, to what in experience has not been, or cannot be, adequately experienced' (ibid.: 540). Importantly, then, this will require a different economy of reading, a reading of that which is missing from the statement. So, for example, as Judith Butler argues, 'it will be one that must be read for what it indicates, but cannot say, or for the unsayable in what is said' (2004b: 156). Ultimately, then, I want to argue for a way of reading that does not follow Young's post-structuralist commitment to the language of discourse, since this requires her to read women's testimony at the express level, whether taken as a statement concerning power or meaning (or more as a statement on the meaning of power, and vice versa), for, as Felman argues, testimony is

> a mode of *truth's realization* beyond what is available as statement, beyond what is available, that is, as a truth transparent to itself and entirely known, given, in advance, prior to the very process of its utterance. The testimony will thereby be understood, in other words, not as a mode of statement of, but rather as a mode of access to, that truth'. (Felman and Laub 1992: 15–16)

Trauma is spoken of only in the moment of testimony: beyond that it is always untold, unspoken, and its truth unknown. In practice, then, if feminists are going to read women's testimony as testimony to trauma they will have to learn to read what is said silently. As Caruth puts it, this is a process of listening to 'the silence of its mute repetition of suffering' (1996: 9). Or as Butler argues, 'One will have to become a reader of the ellipsis, the gap, the absence' or 'broken narratives' (2004b: 155). In sum, a learning to read beyond the economy of overt symptoms or signs, which means, as Hartman puts it, 'more *listening*, more *hearing* of words within words, and a greater openness to *testimony*' (1995: 541).

Suggesting a practice of critical reading based on the reading of 'words within words', silence and ellipsis is, without doubt, a literary conceit, but it is no less 'fanciful' than the theory of critical reading advanced, for example, by Kalí Tal, author of *Worlds of Hurt: Reading the Literatures of Trauma*. Like Young, Tal is interested in how critics read survivor testimony or, as she puts it, the literatures of trauma, asking among other questions: 'What happens when a survivor's story is retold (and revised) by a writer who is not a survivor?' (1996: 3). Of paramount importance for Tal is the meaning the victim intends giving to her experience; indeed, she asserts that there simply are 'meanings available to survivor-readers that are not available to nontraumatised readers', whereupon the non-traumatised reader 'does not have access to the meanings of the sign that invoke traumatic memory' and 'the nontraumatised reader will come away with a different meaning altogether' (ibid.: 16). The literature of trauma is thus 'defined by the identity of its author' (ibid.: 17). This said, however, Tal is, nonetheless, keen to establish that 'The work of the critic of the literature of trauma is both to identify and explicate literature by members of survivor groups' (ibid.: 18). Indeed, she readily acknowledges that the 'reader becomes part of this reconstruction [of the traumatic reality] when she participates in the testimonial process' (ibid.: 203), although for Tal this means: 'I must respect the autonomy of the text; I am a visitor and must observe the requisite courtesies; I must be careful not to appropriate what is not mine' (ibid.: 203). With this warning, Tal advances a series of key principles for reading survivor testimony responsibly.

According to Tal, if we are going to be responsible cultural critics we must meet the following requirements. First, we must contextualise: since it is '[o]nly after we have contextualized the trauma can we separate the outside interpretations of "Other People's Trauma" (OPT) from the narratives of the survivors and successfully "read" the revisions of that trauma' (ibid.: 17). In practice this means that the critic must determine

> the composition of the community of trauma survivors; the nature of the trauma inflicted upon members of the community; the composition of the community of perpetrators; the relationship between the communities of victims and perpetrators; and the contemporary social, political, and cultural location of the community of survivors. (ibid.)

Second, Tal argues it is 'only fair to the reader' if a cultural critic 'provides enough information' about themselves so that the reader can also place them in context (ibid.: 4). Hence, according to Tal, being a responsible cultural critic requires making 'Why me?' integral to one's approach (ibid.: 5). Thus Tal offers a potted history of who she is by making reference to the fact that she is white; Jewish, although raised in an upper-class, secular and 'multiethnic, multiracial extended family'; 'sexually abused as a twelve-year-old by adult friends of my maternal grandfather'; and primarily heterosexual (ibid.: 4).

Third, she writes:

> I believe that the responsibility of the cultural critic is to present a continuous challenge to the assumptions upon which any communal consensus is based – to insist that nothing go without saying. When cultural critics seek to expose and then question the rationales for specific community practices, we situate ourselves in opposition to dominant discourse. We question our own beliefs, and the beliefs of others. We appeal to people's 'good sense,' and we measure our success by the amount of argument we generate. (ibid.: 5)

And finally fourth, 'The involvement of the reader in the testimonial process depends upon her willingness to participate in communal struggle and to identify with the survivor' (ibid.: 203).

There is no doubt in my mind that Tal is making a strenuous and important effort to establish the parameters of reading. But there are clear problems with her recommendations. For surely her demand for contextualisation is prohibitively exhaustive: the composition and relationship of the community of survivors and perpetrators as well as the contemporary social, political, and cultural location of the community of survivors? And, then, the nature of their trauma? And does not her act of contextualising herself not risk being read as a ruse for authorising her reading of testimonies which span a range of traumatic events, including the Holocaust, racial oppression and sexual abuse? This is a point compounded when she asserts that victims of violence constitute a community of readers providing them with privileged access to each other's testimony. And with respect to her third proposition: is not the demand to let 'nothing go without saying' quite simply impossible? Does not the questioning of our beliefs carry the possibility of an endless self-reflexivity? And why must 'we appeal to people's "good sense" ': who are the 'people' and what is 'good sense'? And do we really want to 'measure our success by the amount of argument we generate'? Are there not times when argument generates more heat than light? So despite Tal's caveat that 'such a process is not infinitely reductive, nor does it promote the notion that all theories are equally valid', I am not convinced on the first count, and do not know how to make sense of the second. It is not my intention to make an easy target of Tal's endeavour, but a politics of reading based on the idea that there are 'words within words' appears distinctly less conceited and increasingly modest and prudent when compared to this exorbitant prescription for what constitutes a proper reading of the literatures of trauma.

And finally with respect to Tal's fourth condition: should the reader presume that the survivor wants us to identify with them and partake of their community struggle? Is the presumption of kinship not appropriation in another guise? This is perhaps the most critical question here, precisely because Tal offers her model of reading in opposition to the approach of 'postmodern' readers on the basis that they disregard author intentionality. Thus she argues that the 'approach of most postmodern critics is inappropriate when applied to reading the literature of trauma' because they 'simply claim that an author's intent is irrelevant', which she argues is obviously not how we should approach the literatures of trauma. Whereupon Tal argues, 'The act of *writing*, though perhaps less accessible to the critic, is as important as the act of *reading*' (ibid.: 17–18). Similarly she argues that unlike 'the most playful of the deconstructionists, we do not seek to prove that there is, finally, no solid place to stand' (ibid.: 5). On the question of inappropriate readers, Tal reserves some of her most damning criticism for the psychoanalytical readings of Felman and Laub, whose work represents 'an appropriative gambit of stunning proportions' (ibid.: 54). Felman 'partakes of the worst sort of psychoanalytical pomposity' (ibid.) and her 'hubris' is only matched by the interventionism of Laub and his 'personal appropriative interpretive strategy (ibid.: 56–7, 58). Felman is, she argues, a 'self-styled interpreter', and, as is her habit, Tal adds,

Felman makes 'no distinction between [the] real and the metaphorical' (ibid.: 59).

Tal is not the only critic to take issue with Felman and Laub on the subject of appropriation, but on this score I want to make two final points in this chapter. First, the cogency of claiming that we must not make appropriative readings depends for its force on a set of liberal and deeply individualistic conceits, chief among them being the 'autonomy' or integrity of the testimony. Yet by Tal's own admission the reader is always already part of the process of giving testimony; indeed without a reader there is no testimony. Testimony requires reading, for as Dori Laub argues 'testimonies are not monologues; they cannot take place in solitude' (1992: 70–1) and as Susan Brison argues, 'We are keepers of each other's stories'. But how we receive and 'keep' these stories is open to question, so what I am saying is that we can no longer afford thinking about testimony as the property of the survivor, as her testimony and her testimony alone. For it is only *if* we figure trauma as entering 'the representational field as an expression of personal experience' as Jill Bennett argues, that the question of its vulnerability to 'appropriation, to reduction, and to mimicry' arises in the first instance (2005: 6). Actively interpreting the testimony of others is a political necessity, and this by turn requires a degree of disrespect for its imagined meaning; otherwise there is nothing to read, no reason to interpret 'its' meaning. This said, however, there is disrespect and there is disrespect, hence I would like to invoke, for example, Frigga Haug's notion of 'undogmatic disrespect'; or as Judith Butler puts it in a slightly differently vein: 'a certain respectful dishonouring of intention' (2004: 171). Critical reading, but reading that is 'light' on presumed meaning, and while Tal might object to this proposal, as Ellen Rooney argues 'The check on appropriation and cooptation lies not in some prophylactic disengagement from the stories that are not our's, but from the necessary vulnerability of such a reading to critique, rereading and dismissal' (1996: 16). I can stand corrected.

Second, unlike Tal, I consider there to be merit in taking some lead from the playful deconstructionists. Indeed, I consider there to be value in what Harold Bloom calls a strong misreading, which, as Dominick LaCapra argues, can be understood as a supplement to the method of deconstruction usually associated with Jaques Derrida and Paul de Man (typically understood as a practice of close reading). Denoting a specific relationship between reader and text, LaCapra likens the practice of a strong misreading 'to the "riff" in jazz, wherein one musician improvises on a tune or on the style of an earlier musician' (2000: 44). In practice, however, a strong misreading translates as 'disseminatory writing' (ibid.: 46). 'Dissemination in general', as LaCapra argues,

> supplements deconstruction through an active intervention in which a text is indeed rewritten in terms of possibilities that were underexploited or even unexplored by its author and perhaps remain submerged in the text. [. . .] Its performative quality indicates that it does not simply copy or imitate the manifest content of the text being read but actually makes something happen (or makes history in its own way) through associations and improvisations. (ibid.: 45)

There is a game of language to be played here, which might sound facile, but it is not child's play (or if it is child's play, it is the single most important game to be learnt), for rather than mourn the loss of language as a secure ground for establishing the significance of trauma, we might do better to find new ways of reading the silence left by the experience of violence. For if we do not risk a more adventurous reading, how are we going to make sense of trauma, when, as Tal herself argues, it happens 'outside the bounds of "normal human experience"', so that the 'subject is radically upgrounded' (1996: 15). How are we going to make sense of her following contortion – '[a]ccurate representation of trauma can never be achieved without recreating the event since, by its very definition, trauma lies beyond the bounds of "normal" conception' (ibid.) – without adopting more creative and imaginative ways of reading, ways of reading freed from the conceits that determine what is normal, right and proper? This, however, has always been the feminist challenge in some form or another. So, for example, when writing in the late 1980s, Haug writes:

> Buried or abandoned memories do not speak loudly; on the contrary we can expect them to meet us with obdurate silence. In recognition of this, we must adopt some method of analysis suited to the resolution

of a key question for women; a method that seeks out the un-named, the silent and the absent. (Haug et al. 1987: 65)

She goes on

Here, too, our experience of education maps out a ready-made path of analysis; we have been taught to content ourselves with decoding texts, with searching for truth in textual analysis, complemented at best by the author's own analysis . . . 'Re-learning' in this context means seeing what is not said as interesting, and the fact that it is not said as important, it involves a huge methodological leap, and demands more than a little imagination. (ibid.: 68)

Advocating a strategy of 'light' reading, reading that is light on the word, on the meaning it establishes for the testimony read, is critical if we are to hear the silent past of testimony, for, as Haug also argues, 'alongside omissions, absences and the unnamed, it is still possible to reconstruct past events in the cracks between the echoes of our silence' (ibid.). Importantly, it is time (again) to take a methodological leap, and while Haug was arguing for this leap for different reasons and in relation to differently buried and abandoned memories (as I will discuss more fully in Chapter 4), her analysis finds a resonance here.

To return finally, then, to Tal. While Tal is happy to 'disregard the cultural prohibition against profaning the sacred' in relation to discussing the Holocaust (1996: 8), I would like to apply the same anti-sacral principle to the analysis of sexual abuse and ask that we no longer hold sacred notions of testimony. Indeed, here Judith Herman's formulation of testimony as having 'both a private dimension, which is confessional and spiritual, and a public aspect, which is political and judicial' (1992: 181) is clearly problematic, for when ascribing a sacral dimension to testimony, it becomes difficult to interrogate it without being open to the charge of defiling its integrity. It is time to 'demystify' testimony and the ways in which we can approach it. For when Tal complains that 'Mythologization works by reducing a traumatic event to a set of standardized narratives (twice and thrice-told tales that come to represent "the story" of the trauma)' (ibid.: 6), can she not guess that in repeating the ideological insights of 1970s feminism, she has already told the story twice, and that maybe it is best to develop an alternative language in order not to tell it thrice? Put simply, may it not be better to attempt saying it for the first time, each time, in order to maintain the vitality of political language, to always improvise in the hope that women's testimony might be heard anew?

CHAPTER 2

In All Innocence: Repression and Sylvia Fraser's *My Father's House*

On the front cover of the 1987 Virago edition of Sylvia Fraser's auto-biography, *My Father's House: A Memoir of Incest and of Healing*, there is a family-style snapshot of a little girl standing in a garden. The photograph is a joy to behold, showing the child smiling happily as she squints in the apparent glare of bright summer sunshine. Clutching a doll, dressed in light, frivolous clothes – a short, seem-ingly white, lacy dress and lace knickers showing just beneath her hem – wearing sandals and a ribbon in her hair, she is seen to pose free and easy for the camera. It is a beautiful, mute sepia image which offers us an ordinary, yet apparently idyllic, scene of blissful child-hood, lent greater aura by the fact that it looks like a genuine family photograph, and as such invites speculation as to whether it is a picture of Fraser as a child. For all the world it appears real in every sense: a real photograph and the picture of a really perfect and per-fectly real childhood. The image, it can be said, is the very picture of innocence. But given that the photograph fronts an incest memoir, we know almost immediately it is exactly that: a front, an image that appears to belie the reality it purports to show. The allure of the image shifts dramatically, then, as we imagine that things cannot be what they seem. The appearance of happiness can only be a deception. Thus Fraser's memoir – as graphic testimony to the horrors of incest – works to 'spoil the image' and our pleasures in it. The look of innocent joy is rewritten by the signifying force of incest, and as a consequence we are robbed of the certain knowledge and obvious pleasures served by perceiving her happiness as a reality, faced instead with contemplating a different picture and imagining a harsher truth. The myth, then, no longer holds sway over the image: the image is a fiction. 'How could such innocence be betrayed?' we are left asking by the photograph.

Yet despite this dramatic shift in meaning, the code of innocence remains in place. Whichever way we look at it we see innocence. The innocence of a child and the innocence of a victim. So while her innocence was betrayed by her father, her innocence is redeemed in our eyes. Thus we are a witness to her reality. The look is a compelling one to give. But according to some it is problematic because the scene is rarely as simple as this picture suggests, with a girl standing in all innocence and the perpetrator cast from the scene as the figure of evil; put them together – it has been argued from certain readings of Freud – and the picture is less clear-cut. Put fantasy into the frame, in other words, and things look very different. For years radical feminists have sought to critique the inference of complicity, infantile sexuality, and wish fulfilment held by Freud's reworking of the Oedipal myth. Jeffrey Masson most notably held Freud to account for revising his original seduction theory, whereupon fantasy supplants memory in the aetiology of hysteria so that it has been subsequently argued that women do not repress the shock of an unexpected attack upon their person, but the 'shock' caused by their own, if unconscious, desires and feelings. In sum, they repress the knowledge of an unconscious fantasy, and not the knowledge of a real event, since the former is the source of greater trauma.

This substitution of fantasy for memory as the index of women's traumatic reality has become a highly contested arena of debate, with psychoanalytical feminists persistently arguing in return that Masson's reading of Freud revisions of the seduction theory is a gross simplification which underplays the complex relations of memory, fantasy and reality. So, for example, in a distinctly careful and informed discussion, Ann Scott argues that Masson's account of Freud's repudiation of the seduction theory as a narrative of turning away from memory toward fantasy, and thus an abandoning of the notion of the real event of incest, is already a misinterpretation of the significance of Freud's insights into the interrelationship of these phenomena. Thus she takes issue with Masson's claim that psychoanalysts are interested in only the pathogenic effects of fantasy and not the traumatising effects of real events. She argues, 'Masson is right to say that "psychoanalysts have shown a greater interest in the fantasy life of a patient than in real events" – but only in the sense that psychoanalysts cannot assume that an (external) event bears within it an unalterable (internal) meaning' (1988: 91). Scott, then, goes on to argue, however, that Masson

> mistakenly ascribes to psychoanalysis the view that it is *only* fantasy which has an impact or an effect: indeed that there is no relationship between fantasy and event. In psychoanalysis, however, all events become invested with fantasy, conscious and unconscious, and may on occasion be potentiated *by* fantasy. (ibid.: 91)

These debates, moreover, have become increasingly difficult in light of the false memory syndrome controversy, which I discussed in the last chapter. Indeed, these debates prompted Fraser to publicly condemn the False Memory Syndrome Foundation lobbyists for compounding the problems caused by Freud's original abandonment of his seduction theory, whereupon she accuses them of being 'just like Freud' when he claimed 'that memories of incest developed in therapy are fantasies' (Fraser quoted by Hacking, 1994: 31). In keeping with writers such as Masson, Fraser is obviously keen to uphold the veracity of women's memory to sexual abuse and the historical integrity of the real event, and the aim of this chapter is to lend weight to this effort. This said, however, psychoanalytical feminists are right to claim that traumatic memory and its retrieval are more complex than Masson et al. figure, and I certainly think Scott is right to stress that the value of psychoanalysis is to be found in its refusal to 'assume that an (external) event bears within it an unalterable (internal) meaning', and right also when she claims that 'in Masson there is what I can only call fetishism of the event – that is, of the physical or external event' (ibid.: 97). Thus I agree with Scott that there has been a tendency among feminists following Masson to presume the self-evident and manifest nature of the 'real event'. Indeed, the aim of this book as a whole and this chapter in particular is to rethink the nature of the 'real event', and whether thinking about sexual abuse as an event actually captures its reality. The picture, I want to argue, is not as simple as it looks; the capacity to remember sexual abuse and the significance of the real event is more complex than conventional notions of memory and history might allow.

But the complexity of sexual abuse memory is not, I will stress, a consequence of the role played by fantasy: the unconscious is not sovereign in governing this picture. There are some events that resist fantasy; thus I depart from Scott when she insists on overstating the agency of the unconscious: some events cannot be staged by the work of fantasy. Importantly, then, Scott does not entertain the possibility that some events might escape the powers of the unconscious, which is the point being made by Cathy Caruth when she insists that 'the traumatic symptom cannot be interpreted, simply, as a distortion of reality, nor as the lending of unconscious meaning to a reality it wishes to ignore, nor the repression of what once was wished' (1995: 5). Sexual abuse, it might be argued, is traumatic because it has no meaning for the subject, whether conscious or unconscious. The subject has nothing to say on the matter, not even in or through fantasy. There is, then, more than one way to make the picture complicated, as I will show in this chapter via a reading of Fraser's memoir, although this brings its own problems.

However we might read the picture, the image on the front cover of Fraser's memoir is not a fiction. Life, it seems, is stranger than fiction, by the fact that Fraser lived through her violent childhood as innocently as the image records: she had no idea her father was abusing her, absolutely none. As Fraser puts it:

> I did not remember my daddy ever having touched me sexually. I did not remember ever seeing my daddy naked. I did not remember my daddy ever seeing me naked. In future, whenever my daddy approached me sexually I turned into my other self, and afterwards I did not remember anything that happened. (1987: 15)

As Fraser makes clear here, when she was being abused she turned into somebody else: she 'split', whereupon she was blissfully ignorant of the horrors shaping her life. As she explains it,

> When the conflict caused by my sexual relationship with my father became too acute to bear, I created a secret accomplice for my daddy by splitting my personality in two. Thus, somewhere around the age of seven, I acquired another self with memories and experiences separate from mine, whose existence was unknown to me. (ibid.)

Paradoxically, the image is completely true to her experience: she was a happy child as far as she knew at the time. Something surely happened, but 'Fraser' was not party to it. In a very literal sense, Fraser was not present for her childhood, or rather the violence was taking place without her in attendance. Her life, it seems, was a baffling contradiction, for despite having been subject to years of sexual abuse, Fraser experienced no betrayal of her innocence, which is to say her innocence was not feigned. It was not a pose.

Written after forty years of amnesia, *My Father's House* is a story about the innocence born from living a historically split existence. And as such it is a difficult history for Fraser to negotiate, as, indeed, it is for the reader. Hence, in a note to the reader, Fraser explains that for the sake of clarity she employs a typographically split narrative structure, with italics 'to indicate thoughts, feelings and experiences pieced together from recently recovered memories, and to indicate dreams' (ibid: x). This italicised commentary is designed to convey the story of her 'shadow-twin' who appears sporadically to interrupt and rupture the main narrative. So, for example, she writes:

> Our house is dark [. . .] I bound up the stairs two at a time, fifteen of them, curving around. As my right foot touches the top one, I hear the clearing of a throat. The door to my father's bedroom is open. He calls. I freeze. *My other self lies on her daddy's bed, her arms glued to her sides, her legs numb. For the first time penetration is attempted, though it is by no means completed.* (ibid.: 43)

The italics represent her recovered memories of childhood, or, as Fraser puts it, the italics represent the 'voice of [her] other self chiming in' with her 'nast[y] contrapuntal' (ibid.: 77).

The significance of this conceit has been the subject of a range of commentary. So, for example, Christine Clegg argues that it is helpful in providing Fraser with a 'means of establishing a distinction between the conventional narration of a knowable life history, and the fiction of an unconscious history' (1999: 75), whereupon Clegg argues '*My Father's House* can be read as an exemplary text, both in relation to the formation and circulation of a genre, and for the ways in which it is also so clearly caught between the acts of witnessing and creative writing' (ibid.: 70). According to Suzette Henke, Fraser, a creative writing teacher, 'carefully circumnavigates the highly contested territory of recovered memory' (1998: 121–2). Henke thus maintains that by 'typographically distinguishing between autobiographical discourse and imaginary projections (or reconstructions) that occupy a liminal space between fantasy and reality', Fraser 'protects herself, at least theoretically, from accusations of "false memory syndrome"' (ibid.: 122). 'By attributing recovered data to the realm of the imaginary,' Henke continues, Fraser is

> free to explore the fertile terrain of dream and childhood recollection without subjecting herself to the kind of sceptical scrutiny that currently surrounds adult confessions of repressed trauma. 'Whether you believe me or not,' she seems to be saying, 'I know what I experienced.' Her narrative proves so vivid and convincing that we, as readers, do indeed believe her. (ibid.)

In spite of Henke's resolute optimism concerning reader response, Fraser's narrative has not proved so vivid and convincing that all readers have duly believed her. Or, rather, for some readers it is precisely because it 'so vivid and convincing' that they have chosen to subject it to 'the kind of sceptical scrutiny that currently surrounds' recovered memory testimony. Thus the creativity that Clegg and Henke applaud has become the focus of considerable debate. Despite Fraser's desire to quell anxiety over the authenticity of her testimony – which she does in no uncertain terms when she concludes in a note to the reader, 'That my father did sexually abuse me has been corroborated by outside sources. Our family secret, it appears, was not such a secret after all' (1987: x) – she cannot secure its status as a report on history. In the end, and again despite claiming that to her knowledge she has 'not exaggerated or distorted or misrepresented the truth' as she 'now understand[s] it' (ibid.), Fraser can do nothing to settle the questions that always come to haunt a claim to repressed sexual trauma: is it real? Is it really possible to forget that you were repeatedly abused and raped throughout your childhood? Surely, if it had actually happened, it would be impossible to forget? Unforgettable? Is it not the case, then, that the girl was as happy as the photograph shows and the rest is fiction? Fantasy? For surely no one can be as innocent as all that?

These questions over where autobiography ends and fiction begins are not unique to Fraser's memoir of repressed incest, since, as Leigh Gilmore argues in her book *The Limits of Autobiography*, there has always been a general question over women's life writing and a general question over the writing of any history of violence. But as Gilmore goes on to argue in her discussion of Dorothy Allison's incest 'novel' *Bastard out of Carolina*, while the question of the limits of autobiography is a generic one, it belies other questions 'that call our attention to how hard it is to tell the story of trauma', whereupon Gilmore argues that

> the initial question 'Where does autobiography end and fiction begin' can be reformulated as a struggle between what is real and what is imagined in the representation of the self and trauma. At stake is how antagonistic the monitoring of the real will be to the presence of the imagined. (2001: 46)

Significantly, Gilmore is not only drawing our attention to the ways in which the author might have to struggle with establishing what might figure as real and what might figure as imaginary (a struggle that the author might pass on to the reader), but more precisely she is drawing our attention to how the real itself might resist representation (a struggle less likely, if not impossible, to pass on to the reader). The presence of the imagined might not be sufficient to monitor the real. Thus while fiction may be readily called to mediate the real, it may find itself stalled in its efforts: 'No narrative is easy to tell' (ibid.: 46). Hence Fraser's creative writing skills might yet be beside the point, for, as Gilmore argues, 'Trauma emerges in narrative as much through what cannot be said of it as through what can' (ibid.). Or, indeed, more poignantly: 'If your "story" is the one no one wants to hear and which cannot be told given certain rules and expectation about form, then silence is your sentence' (ibid.: 63).

In the context of Fraser's life, the idea that 'silence is your sentence' has profound resonance, historically and grammatically. Historically, because Fraser was condemned to be silent, not simply because incest was an unspeakable violence in the social-historical context of 1950s Canada. Nor because her father would threaten her with repercussions if she said anything. But because the violence rained on her left her at a complete loss for words, so that her father's subsequent demands for silence were already redundant: she had nothing to say away. No one to split on, not even herself at this point.

Her sentence was, indeed, to remain silent. Grammatically, once left speechless, there is no option but to speak silently of the horrors you have witnessed – in saying nothing Fraser was saying everything she could about the horror of her life. This is 'illegitimate' testimony, which means, as Gilmore argues, grammatically incorrect speech (ibid.: 67); silence it might be said is poor grammar, or else speech contravening the rules of grammar; it cannot be said properly and thereby no one is likely to hear you, let alone listen to you.

Following Gilmore and like so many others concerned with the writing of trauma, I am keen to mark Fraser's creative attempt to 'work herself into the symbolic' (ibid.), for, as Gilmore maintains, 'The ability to write beyond the silencing meted out by trauma is an achievement' (ibid.: 24). But I am also wary of how this is done, for all too often it requires a prioritising of literary prowess. So, for example, Gilmore privileges what formal innovation can tell about the representation of trauma over and above the register of less formally innovative testimony, hence her enquiry is about what 'formal experimentation make[s] visible that repetition alone – telling another trauma story – may not' (ibid.: 48–9). 'To be sure', she adds,

> repetition is valuable and the compilation of additional testimonies of trauma is important in all sorts of areas: establishing that injuries occurred, documenting abuse, deepening existing accounts, extending traditions of reporting and testimony. This is cultural work that must be nurtured and continued. At the same time, an alternative and allied discourse of trauma that draws on less familiar (and authorized) forms of reporting risks in documentary believability what it recoups in a reconception of the subject of trauma. (ibid.: 49)

Leaving aside the question of whether or not repetition achieves what Gilmore suggests it does, if trauma provokes a crisis representation, caution must be exercised when ascribing so-called experimental forms with a power to render visible what conventional narrative cannot. Experimental fiction is no more or less language bound than conventional testimony, and thereby it offers no more or less privileged access to the truth of trauma. In addition, also, Gilmore's stress on experimental writing serves to privilege the

powers of the author, when trauma, as I understand it, puts author-
ial power in crisis. Thus despite the possessive quality of the statement 'silence is your sentence', my understanding would be that
trauma institutes a break such that there is every possibility that you
are left with a silence severed from an enabling sentence. True
silence, without its being known as such. So, there might yet be
another story told by *My Father's House*, a silent one undetected by
Fraser but one that might still be read as speech. I should stress it is
not my intention to eulogise silence as marking the site of trauma
and thus a redeeming conceit. Silence is not truth. But rather if
silence is your sentence it can be thought of as an ordinary, desper-
ately mundane, badly strung sentence, if bearing within it extraordinary implications for the ways in which we think about and read
trauma testimony. In sum, despite Clegg's and Henke's commentary
on Fraser's achievement, *My Father's House* is not a creative piece of
testimony; and despite Margaret Atwood claiming on the back cover
that *My Father's House* is 'beautiful[ly] written', I find it lacks the
kind of eloquence and fluency implied by beauty: *My Father's House*
is, at best, an ugly story, if a story written at all.

What, then, is the story? In a frequently commented upon note to
the reader, Fraser claims from the very beginning of her memoir that
'The story I have told is autobiographical'. This sentence introduces
My Father's House, and it asserts that the book conforms to the
expectations of genre: it *is* autobiography. It is read as saying: 'This
is my autobiography', which, as Gilmore argues, is the genre in
which

> a person, solid and incontestable, testifies to having lived. An autobi-
> ography is a monument to the idea of personhood, to the notion that
> one could leave behind a memorial to oneself [. . .] and that the
> memorial would perform the work of permanence that the person
> never can. A self-memorial says: 'I remember, and now, so will you.'
> (ibid.: 12–13)

Or, as she notes later, autobiography is the literary moment of
American individualism which is informed by the 'democratic ide-
ology of *e pluribus unum*. Stand up, it says, and represent yourself.
Or, sit back and designate someone else to represent you' (ibid.: 19).

But Fraser's claim to writing an autobiography is not a declarative statement of this order: it appears hesitant – 'The *story* I have told is autobiographical'. Why, then, on reading *My Father's House* are we struck by a note of uncertain definition? Of course, it is easy and in some measure correct to suggest that this hesitancy reflects the anxiety any woman might feel when writing an incest memoir, given myths concerning sexual abuse, including the idea that young girls court the attention of their fathers, albeit unconsciously and in all innocence. And certainly Fraser knows this to be a pernicious myth, making reference to it in her memoir when describing the reception of *Pandora's Box*, her first book, published in 1972. Based on the story of forty years of a woman's life – Pandora's – the book includes a scene of near sexual assault. This scene becomes the focus of discussion when she is being interviewed about the book by an old school friend named as Joker. In the first instance Joker asks her whether or not she had experienced anything of the sort. Fraser concedes no real knowledge of what it must be like to be a victim of sexual abuse: as she puts it, 'I wouldn't know how to write about a kid as emotionally damaged as that' (1987: 158). Thereby Joker challenges the plausibility of sexual assault, charging Fraser with weaving 'a web of innocence around the child', whereby he insists 'we must look at the conduct of the child' and 'little girls can be seductive at an early age' (ibid.). 'I think your book', Joker says to Fraser, 'is typical of the kind of hysterical imaginings we're seeing too much of these days' (ibid.). Eleven years later Fraser's encounter with Joker returns to haunt her, when she hears that Joker has sexually assaulted a girl. This is the pivotal moment in *My Father's House* because it triggers a returning sense of what had happened. ' "I think my father raped me", she tells a friend. "Is that supposed to be a joke?" her friend replies. "I didn't know what I was going to say till I heard myself. Now I think it's true" ' (ibid.: 220). Whereupon she has her first memory of being orally raped, forty years after the act of violence.

My Father's House is built on a perhaps more incredible, or at least distinctly more complex, conceit than that of attempting to establish the reality of incest for a potentially hostile audience, for she is writing of that which 'was unknown' to her for most of her life up to that point. For over four decades, Fraser had no memory of the abuse, having dissociated at the point when her 'helplessness is so bottom-less that anything is preferable' (ibid.: 221). As she writes:

> I gag. I'm smothering. Help me! I scrunch my eyes so I can't see. My daddy is pulling my body over him like mommy pulls a holey sock over a darning egg. Filthy, filthy don't ever let me catch you shame shame filthy daddy won't love me love me dirty filthy love him hate him fear don't fear ever let me catch you dirty dirty love hate guilty shame *fear fear fear fear fear fear*. (ibid.: 220–1)

How, then, to write this story as an autobiography when the subject's ability to maintain any sense of conscious awareness or commentary gives way to streaming incomprehension, until finally, when fear supplants all hope of possible reason, the subject splits from the scene of her life. What happens, then, to the capacity to narrate an autobiography when it is a genre based on the possibility of 'a person, solid and incontestable' testifying 'to having lived'? How does a victim experiencing the levels of depersonalisation 'felt' by Fraser write 'a monument to the idea of personhood'? How do you write your autobiography when strictly it is a biography, but not the biography of someone who may, indeed, seem very real, but of someone who is barely real to you, for, as Fraser puts it, not only was this other her 'shadow-twin', but at times also she passed like a figure in dream? Put succinctly, then, how do you write your story when it appears like a dream or else stranger than fiction? Its author split by her experiences of sexual abuse, *My Father's House* begins as a question of storytelling because it could not have been anything but a story for Fraser for nigh on forty years, no more real than *Pandora's Box* was when she wrote it eleven years before her first memory. As a life story, it is impossible to write.

But does this reading quell the question of fantasy? The answer, of course, is no, or certainly it is no if you are reading Elaine Showalter's *Hystories: Hysterical Epidemics and Modern Culture*, which represents a blatantly provocative attempt on her part to promote the political importance of Freud's work on hysteria. 'A century after Freud', Showalter begins, 'people [still] reject psychological explanations for symptoms; they believe psychosomatic disorders are illegitimate and search for physical evidence that firmly places cause and cure outside the self' (1997: 4). According to Showalter, people are willing only to look outside themselves to explain what lies within. Hence Showalter maintains that we are now witnessing a tide of 'hysterical epidemics'. Controversially, these epidemics are named by her as chronic fatigue, Gulf War syndrome, recovered memory of sexual abuse, multiple personality disorders, satanic ritual abuse, and alien abduction, four of which she readily admits can be cross-referenced in terms of sexual abuse. Indeed, given the fact that she slips anorexia and bulimia into her discussion of the above six psychogenic syndromes, which again are understood by her to be referenced in terms of childhood sexual abuse, it is apparent that childhood sexual abuse is the common denominator for Showalter. However, leaving this aside for the moment, we are living, Showalter is keen to assert, in a 'hot zone of psychogenic diseases': 'psychological plagues' which are 'all too real', yet remain misdiagnosed as externally caused (ibid.: 4). Or perhaps more precisely, and certainly put more precisely than Showalter manages, because they are experienced as 'real' they are not readily thought of as psychological in origin. According to Showalter, then, 'Contemporary hysterical patients blame external sources – a virus, sexual molestation, chemical warfare, satanic conspiracy, alien infiltration – for psychical problems' (ibid.).

This said, however, Showalter is keen not to be misunderstood, hence she maintains:

> We need not assume that patients are either describing an organic disorder or else lying when they present similar narratives of symptoms. Instead, patients learn about diseases from the media, unconsciously develop symptoms, and then attract media attention in an endless cycle. The human imagination is not infinite, and we are bombarded by these plot lines every day. Inevitably, we all live out the social stories of our time. (ibid.: 6)

The contemporary hysteric – figured here as a sufferer of any of the epidemics outlined above – is not being deceitful or else suffering from something thought to have happened to them, but rather they are necessarily living out today's story, although critically for Showalter today's story is one of 'denial, projection, accusation and blame' (ibid.: x). We are not willing, according to Showalter, to accept responsibility for ourselves and our actions, choosing instead to look elsewhere for the source of our condition; we want to figure ourselves as victims so we can absolve ourselves of responsibility. In short, we are not willing to accept or contemplate the place of virulent fantasies in our life, preferring instead to imagine ourselves as the unwilling, innocent subjects of other toxic agents, human and non-human.

Fraser figures among the people Showalter is complaining about when Showalter reads *My Father's House* as a 'hystory' – which is to say a hysterical narrative caused by intrapsychical conflict – and not a testimony to sexual abuse. Showalter writes:

> Under hypnosis with a sympathetic therapist Fraser recovered memories of abuse, which explains to her satisfaction why she has never been completely happy and why she had an affair that ended her marriage to a decent, loving man. Since her therapist believed that child abuse often leads to multiple personality syndrome, he encouraged Fraser to locate her other self [. . .]
>
> It is the other self, Fraser tells us who is writing the book: 'My other self has learned to type. She presses keys, throwing up masses of defiant memories.' 'Imagine this,' she concludes, 'imagine you discover that for many years another person intimately shared your life without you knowing it.' Fraser does not have dramatic or even visible symptoms of either *grande* or *petite hystérie*. But she cannot accept responsibility for the affair that destroyed her marriage; she blames the affair on her other self. 'It wasn't so much passion that tempted me,' Fraser writes, 'but compulsion that drove her. Like a sleepwalker I watched askance while someone who looked like me cast aside everything I valued to recreate an infantile world in which no will or desire existed outside of the illicit affair.' In order to account for the adulterous affair, Fraser must posit an incestuous relationship with Daddy. Actually she never quite remembers the incest, but she knows it happened. It must have, for otherwise why wouldn't she be happy? Why wouldn't she be faithful? Seeing herself as a victim allows Fraser to forgive herself for the infidelity, for the damage to her husband, who died soon after the divorce, and even for writing books. (ibid.: 165)

Constituting her complete 'reading' of Fraser's memoir, Showalter's summary analysis is replete with basic inaccuracies, most notably that Fraser does claim that as a child she had violent convulsions, which were witnessed at the time and later confirmed by her sister. And as such these could easily be read as both a dramatic and visible symptom of *grande hystérie*, thereby serving as the evidence Showalter takes to be missing from her account. But neither textual nor historical accuracy is Showalter's concern since she is reading *My Father's House* as a culturally expedient fiction and not as testimony to sexual abuse, thus exemplifying her claim that 'similarities between two stories do not mean that they mirror a common reality' (ibid.: 6). *My Father House's* might read like a report on the memory of incest but it is, in fact, a 'crafted and very literary' piece of work (ibid.: 166). Unlike Henke, then, who considers the very textuality of *My Father's House* as a creative attempt to secure a safe place for exploring traumatic memories, for Showalter *My Father's House* is designed for expiating guilt. For Showalter, then, and without apparent equivocation, the 'real' motivation for Fraser's memoir is a presumed desperate, because socially unacceptable, sense of guilt at having sexually transgressed. Thus Fraser is figured as having to conjure a history of child sexual abuse as a means of alleviating the guilt felt for incurring the moral debt of infidelity. (If it were not for the fact that Showalter is so cavalier in dismissing Fraser's history of sexual abuse, her commentary could be read rhetorically as a demonstration of the levels of guilt women incur when they do have affairs. This would explain why Showalter figures Fraser as guilty not only for the affair, and thus responsible for both the damage caused her husband and by implication his death 'soon after' – in fact after a gap of ten years, during which he remarried and had children – but also for writing, which means ultimately that women are held guilty for any form of self-expression, sexual or textual. If not taken too seriously, and read as spoof, Showalter might be said to have a point.)

At stake for Showalter is not that Fraser has had an affair but that there is no cultural tolerance for her doing so, hence her need to posit an external cause for the havoc she has caused, but cannot culturally accept. To this end, Fraser is a hysteric in Freud's revised sense in that she is repressing culturally forbidden desires. At this point, however, Showalter is 'careful' to establish she does not 'regard hysteria as weakness, badness, feminine deceitfulness, or irresponsibility, but rather a cultural symptom of anxiety and stress. The conflicts that produce hysterical symptoms are genuine and universal; hysterics are not liars and therapists are not villains' (ibid.: 9). Again she writes:

> Hysteria is neither the sign of a higher consciousness nor the badge of a shameful weakness. Women still suffer from hysterical symptoms not because we are essentially irrational or because we're all victims of abuse but because, like men, we are human beings who will convert feelings into symptoms when we are unable to speak – when, for example, we feel overwhelmed by shame, guilt, or helplessness. (ibid.: 205)

At issue, then, is not the recovery of memory, but the illicit desire provoking a sense of personal trauma. Put conversely, it is only by imagining herself as a victim that she can culturally accept responsibility for her actions: her agency is no agency. For this reason, then, Showalter deplores 'the credulous endorsement of recovered memory' (ibid.: 11) and argues:

> Feminists have an ethical as well as an intellectual responsibility to ask tough questions about the current narratives of illness, trauma, accusation, and conspiracy. We have a responsibility to address the problems behind the epidemics – including the need to protect children from sexual and physical abuse. (ibid.: 13)

Despite her apparently sincere caveat concerning the need to protect children from abuse, Showalter's book has generated outrage – which is hardly surprising, given her flagrant and outright disregard for Fraser's history of abuse, a reading Showalter can get away with only because she is prepared to so brazenly exploit the fact that Fraser can never prove her claims, since this proof lies outside the text. Thus Fraser is left no where and with no ground(s) to write her story of abuse. Outside confirmation of the reality of the event can never be secured by the autobiography, a point known only too well by Showalter: hence ultimately her desire to 'lead the way in making distinctions between metaphors and realities, between therapeutic narratives and destructive hystories' (ibid.: 13) is disingenuous, to say the least. (Again I am tempted to adopt Showalter's own logic when she suggests 'similarities between two stories do not mean that they mirror a common reality' to therefore read *Hystories* less as a seriously meant commentary on the fantasy status of Fraser's claim to sexual abuse, but rather as a parody of how it could be read if Fraser's claims were, indeed, not given credibility. In other words, if Showalter's *Hystories* is itself a piece of hysterical writing, as others have suggested, it is by its very nature duplicitous and can be read alternatively as saying what it does not mean.)

Hystories has, as I have just noted, provoked an enraged response which Showalter appears to take pleasure in. So, for example, she recalls how when she gave a talk about recovered memory at the Dartmouth School of Criticism and Theory in the summer of 1994 – when I might add the controversy over false memory syndrome was running at its height – she was met with anger and distress, and was asked 'to take the chapter out of [her] book' (ibid.: 157–8). 'They looked stunned', Showalter writes, 'when I said that, on the contrary, I planned to expand it' (ibid.). To which she adds:

> of course, the sexual, physical, and emotional abuse of children is a terrible reality. My quarrel in this book is not with the realities of child abuse, or the vigorous investigation of *children's* complaints, but with the ideologies of recovered memory and the process of accusation based on adult therapy. (ibid.: 158)

In other words, children might speak of incest as long as their testimony is vigorously vetted, but women can never speak of testimony (having grown up to become hysterics). Showalter writes: 'I have come to doubt the validity of therapeutically recovered memories of sexual abuse, but I do not wish to belittle those who believe in their memories. People do not generate these confabulations out of an intention to deceive. They may need to define an identity, to work out anger towards the accused, or to respond to cultural pressures' (ibid.: 147). In sum, they are hysterics in an unEnlightened postmodern world.

Whatever else she might be arguing, Showalter clearly wishes to stoke the debate over Freud's legacy, and has thus generated perhaps more interesting commentary from other psychoanalytically informed feminist readers keen to demonstrate that the debate over hysteria's aetiology and the value of Freud's turn towards fantasy is more complex than Showalter's polemic allows – or at least this is the conclusion reached by Susannah Radstone (1999) in her critically temperate review of Showalter's book. Offering a useful clarification of feminist attachment to the idea of fantasy, Radstone begins by arguing that the shift executed by Freud from memory to fantasy can be seen as that which 'reveals psychoanalysis's strivings to bring hysterical (and other neurotic) symptoms under the sway of the subject's (albeit unconscious) determinations, and, with analytic aid, modifications, rather than to consign them to the paradoxical intractability and volatility of memory's relation to events' (1999: 245). Key, here, for Radstone, as indeed it is for Scott, is the idea that fantasy holds open a place for agency against or in spite of the 'intractability and volatility of memory's relation to events'. For Radstone, memory works to cancel the possibility of agency or, at least, delimit it, whereas fantasy works to free us, not the converse as would be suggested by Masson, for example. According to Radstone, then, fantasy does not institute the radical foreclosure of historical agency, but is its condition of possibility. Summarising the terms of this debate, Radstone thus asserts that for Masson and those following his suit, such as Herman, fantasy is understood not to be 'a potential expansion of the capacity to grasp and act in and upon "reality"', but as 'the striking out of the historical reality of abuse' (ibid.: 246). Radstone holds the view that memory requires fantasy to achieve its historical potential, that we require fantasy to be historical subjects in the first instance.

In light of this emphasis on the historical agency established by fantasy, Radstone argues that:

> For Showalter, hystories appear to represent a withdrawal from the hard task enjoined by [Freud's] insights: that of grasping as our own unconscious fantasies the violent, destructive, or sexual forces that hystories locate and persecute elsewhere and in others. Showalter's impassioned plea is both a *cri du cœur* and an unashamed appeal for a return to enlightenment values. [. . .] Thus if the Freudian turn can be narrativized as a politically progressive one, then Showalter's thesis follows that Enlightenment tradition. For it is the recognition of *universal* human propensities and, in particular, the grasping of responsibility for our own projections that promises to move us beyond a culture of blame inhabited by perpetrators and victims, and towards a freer and more equal society. (ibid.: 248–9)

On this reading, it is possible to say that Radstone's review of *Hystories* does well to establish why Showalter's wild polemic might be considered a progressive rhetoric as opposed to the reactionary tracts of FMSF lobbyists, such as the one offered by Frederick Crews, whom I discussed in the last chapter, since at issue, as read by Radstone, are the possibilities held for women by instituting a place for unconscious agency.

This said, however, Radstone is also critical of Showalter because her

> eschewal of memory in favour of fantasy appears also to have produced an eschewal of history. To be more accurate, it eschews the possibility that the relation between the inner and the external worlds – between the psychical and the historical – may be more two-way than her thesis would seem to allow. (ibid.: 250)

Importantly, Radstone is looking to move feminist psychoanalytical thinking beyond the impasse established by the likes of Masson and Showalter. It is not memory or fantasy, but rather fantasy has a say in history, and history has a say in fantasy. According to Radstone, then,

> Showalter's exclusive focus on fantasy leaves [her] uneasy, for history has its responsibility and burden too: to bear witness to traces of 'happenings' which leave their traumatic and enigmatic marks upon the memories of peoples and individuals, *Hystories'* theoretical substitution of fantasy for memory splits fantasy too violently from history and memory, thus (paradoxically) risking repeating trauma's violent cut. (ibid.: 251)

Thus Radstone concludes that the task 'is to conceptualise culture and history itself not in terms of the false dichotomy of memory or fantasy, but as the enigmatic inter weaving of the traces deposited by both' (ibid.: 252).

Radstone's acknowledgement of the limits of Showalter's position is, of course, a welcome one, not least because, as she argues, a 'psychoanalytically "correct" concentration on the inner world's capacity to shape the sense made of the outer world tips over into what looks like a refusal to acknowledge that the external world can have *any* determining force whatsoever' (ibid.: 251). Given that she is reviewing Showalter's *Hystories*, it is not the place for Radstone to elaborate on her ideas, but elsewhere she argues that Freud's concept of *Nachträglichkeit* is key to how we might reconceptualise culture and history 'as the enigmatic inter weaving of the traces deposited by both [memory and fantasy]'. Indeed, without an understanding of this concept it is not possible, she argues, to grasp the genuine lasting significance of psychoanalytic insight into the interrelationship of memory and fantasy, which she argues is not merely a question of the mediating role played by fantasy. But as she stresses, 'The psychoanalytic understanding of memory encompasses two related fields: those of temporality and symbolisation' (2000: 85). There is here then,

> a dual emphasis on temporality and textuality such that each render the activity of the other radically opaque. So, for example, it is only by ignoring psychoanalytical insight into temporality that it is possible to imagine that 'memories' condensations and displacements might then be interpreted to uncover what has been repressed in the experience of an event. (ibid.)

According to Radstone, then, 'psychoanalytic insights concerning the marks left by repression' do not alone disrupt 'history's model of narrative, which posits a chain of events occurring in linear time and linked by cause and effect' (ibid.). This model is put into question only by 'the psychoanalytical understanding of the temporality of the unconscious' – an understanding she argues that 'hinges on the concept of *Nachträglichkeit*, or 'afterwardsness' (Laplanche 1992)' (ibid.).

Translating this concept as a process of 'deferred revision', Radstone maintains that it temporalises our understanding of the production of memory by emphasising the role played by present concerns. As she puts it, 'The proposal that "memories" of the past are shaped by more recent experiences reverses history's model of cause and effect, by making the present, to some extent, the "cause" of memory's representations of the past' (ibid.: 85–6).

> In place of the quest for the truth of an event, and the history of its causes, *Nachträglichkeit* proposes, rather, that the analysis of memory's tropes can reveal not the truth of the past, but a particular

revision prompted by later events, thus pitting psychical contingency against historical truth. (ibid.: 86)

Speaking psychoanalytically, the present is seen to precede the past, which is revised to fit with present-day concerns, desires and understandings (most of which are not known consciously). As a consequence of adopting a concept of *Nachträglichkeit*, it is no longer possible to explore memory in terms of the question of the truth of its past: rather, memory is only ever a function of the present conditions under which it emerges. The past, in other words, exists only in the service of the present-day subject, if symbolically veiled.

This said, however, for Radstone, the question of the status of the past is more permanently and structurally deferred than this account has suggested so far, because not only are the memories of the past the product of contemporary desires, fantasies and motivations, but they are also more likely to be linked with 'primal *fantasies* than with historical reality' (ibid.: 86). According to Radstone the idea of the primal fantasy is radical since it implies two things. First, she argues, 'it suggests that inner reality is shaped by certain unchanging, universal and ahistorical fantasies related to human sexuality' (ibid.: 86). And second, it suggests 'a view of inner reality within which desires and fantasies that run counter to conscious control hold sway' (ibid.). So while psychoanalysis establishes a relationship between 'events and memory', the positing of a primal fantasy complicates 'any attempt to map memory straightforwardly onto events, since it adds to the view of memory as the later revision of events, the proposal that those revisions are inextricably woven with fantasy' (ibid.). On this view, traumatic symptoms emerge where a seemingly innocuous event prompts '*memories* of an earlier event that now becomes associated with inadmissible *fantasies*' (ibid.). Thus, Radstone argues that the question of pathology 'derives not from the remembered event itself but from the attempt to defend against the fantasies that now emerge in association with such memories' (ibid.: 87). Consequently, this means that traumatic memory cannot be understood 'as the registration of an event, but as the outcome of a complex process of revision shaped by promptings from the present' (ibid.: 89). In the strongest possible sense, the past alone does not exist for Radstone. Trauma is not a question of the repression of history but a question of the 'repression of fantasy' (ibid.: 88), with the unwanted fantasy triggered by the 'original' traumatic event, all of which is worked over in the present. Memory on this account is radically non-linear and inseparable from fantasy.

Although *Nachträglichkeit* is being used by Radstone to introduce a notion of history into a psychoanalytical reading of memory, there is no doubt that fantasy retains the greater say. Fantasy, it appears, is always already on hand to dictate the shape of our memories and to supply meaning to the events that shape our lives and thereby produce us as historical subjects; it appears always already to be the occasion of memory, forever the sovereign agent of memory and historical subjectivity. Is there, then, no history or memory on which fantasy is lost? No moment in which psychic agency is completely stalled? No history that is not freighted with ancient fantasy? No memory that cannot be subordinated to the bidding of the present-day subject? Are there not times when trauma can be explained only by the 'intractability and volatility of memory's relation to events'? On this reading, there appears little evidence to suggest the contrary, despite Radstone's critique of Showalter and her express desire to afford history and memory a place in psychoanalysis. So does *Nachträglichkeit* really offer the advance on hysteria that Radstone suggests?

This question can be answered by exploring Nicola King's reading of *My Father's House*. As stated by King, then, Fraser's story is written according to 'the trope of repression and recovery, the rediscovery of the buried past' (2000: 8), but by deploying the concept of *Nachträglichkeit* King sets out to demonstrate that while Fraser might maintain that her narrative is an accurate re-creation or reconstruction of her past,

> the structure she has produced is so highly and tightly constructed, and the recovery and representation of memory so apparently complete, that doubts arise about the truth status of the events she reconstructs and the appropriateness of these novelistic techniques for this material. (ibid.: 62)

In keeping with Showalter, King finds the very literary nature of Fraser's autobiography raises questions about the authenticity of her memories, once again demonstrating the limits of Henke's view that Fraser's narrative 'proves so vivid and convincing that we, as readers, do indeed believe her'. Thus King argues that Fraser's revelatory scene of remembering the oral rape, 'which is prepared for by means of an intricately plotted chain of events and coincidences', may make for an unconvincing read if plotted as fiction, but if plotted as a memoir this sense of implausibility will engender 'doubt about the truth of the events being narrated' (ibid.: 64). It is, in other words, too neat, too tidy, too over determined, for the air of truth. It is also, she argues, too detailed for life:

> Paradoxically, the 'thickening' of detail which provides the texture of reality in a novel seems unconvincing in a text which purports to be autobiographical, and is problematised even further when much of the narrator's past was supposedly forgotten for forty years. Fraser's use of the 'techniques of the novelist' evades the question of the unreliability, fluidity and 'retranscription' of memory. (ibid.)

By borrowing the techniques of the novelist, Fraser has ended up telling a somewhat bad story, and one that trades structurally on the 'thrill' afforded a plot building towards a shocking denouncement. As King argues, because

> the narrator is telling her story from the beginning with the full knowledge which she has acquired by the end, [the] hints [of sexual abuse] function as a kind of titillation, the promise of further shocking details to come. Full narrative gratification is thus postponed until near the end of the text, when Fraser finally remembers. (ibid.: 68–9)

Indeed, according to King, the plotting of *Pandora* as the trigger for the 'chain of events which leads to the revelation of the truth about her past, [is] the most contrived and novelistic aspect of the text' (ibid.). 'It is this kind of narrative coincidence which makes the reader aware of the construction of a sequence of events almost too tightly plotted to be convincing as truth' (ibid.: 81).

It is safe to say, then, that King is not convinced, especially when Fraser is writing up her dreams 'in which the events and images of her life are reworked and represented in a way which symbolise the hidden truth in a manner almost too direct to be plausible', and 'whose obvious symbolic content makes them difficult to credit if we are reading the text as autobiography', with one dream in particular 'too obvious to need interpretation, and [giving] the unfortunate impression of having been invented for the purpose' (ibid.: 83). And again,

> Fraser does recover memory independently of her dreams, but they are so tightly constructed, or reconstructed, and so obviously symbolic, that it often seems as if they have been either dreamed in response to recovered memory or even constructed in order to provide evidence for it. (ibid.)

If Fraser is figuring as a second-rate novelist, she also figures as a second-rate analyst. She reads her dreams too literally, while writing too obviously.

At issue for King is, however, a perhaps more serious point, and hence her intention is not simply to critique Fraser for writing and reading her life badly: rather, King is concerned by her efforts to conceal the constructed nature of all memory and thus mask the impossibility of her typographical conceit which purports to give an unreconstructed account of her past, uncontaminated by contemporary understanding. But as King argues, it is impossible to hold 'apart the memory of an event and its interpretation' (ibid.: 78). The 'truth' about the preserved and rediscovered past only emerges as an effect of narrative itself' (ibid.: 62), which is written very much in and from the present. 'Past and present cannot be held apart, in spite of the narrative strategies used by [. . .] Fraser in an attempt to do so' (ibid.: 65). The present will rush in to write the past: the 'fact that both italics and roman are used for the interpretation of past experience is a textual acknowledgement of what the text otherwise denies, that memory as such cannot always be distinguished from the ongoing process of "translation"' (ibid.: 66). Accordingly, King is looking to establish the influence of the present concerns over the past, and the instability and uncertainties this brings to the process of remembering, a recognition not provided by Fraser. The problem with *My Father's House* is it lacks recognition of its own desire; Fraser demonstrates no 'idea of memory and identity as a continual process of "retranslation"' and she does not 'acknowledge the provisionality and incompleteness of memories of childhood' (ibid.: 61). For King, then, *My Father's House* is just a little too mechanical, too contrived, a little too neat to register as true.

But King does not simply query the plausibility of Fraser's memoir on narrative grounds alone. Her critique is substantive as well as formal. Thus she queries the plausibility of Fraser's claim to amnesia. According to King, Fraser's claim to have lived a split existence with 'her other self' taking responsibility for the knowledge of the abuse is also problematic for the reader since they are 'also being asked to accept this "other self" as a psychic reality, "constructed" by the psyche as a defence mechanism in response to the radical assault on the child's sense of self' (ibid.: 71). 'The creation of this other self could be interpreted', King argues, 'as a response to trauma which the psyche cannot register', or a 'supposed defence against an intolerable reality' (ibid.), but as her qualifying emphases suggest, this is not the interpretation favoured by King. Indeed, she expresses considerable doubt as to whether anyone can claim 'amnesia' for forty years:

> Although survivors of accidents or violent assaults often attest to a 'blacking out' of some details of the traumatic event, 'amnesia' is the kind of forgetting which few survivors or therapists claim or describe, talking in terms of isolated and often meaningless visual images which cannot be articulated, or affectless narratives which hold memory at a distance. (ibid.: 65)

So while the 'repression of the memory of a few isolated incidents of infantile abuse' might be 'easier to accept than the idea of the conscious and repeated repression of the knowledge and memory of a more or less continuous experience' (ibid.: 76), how might we understand Fraser's amnesia if it does not represent the repression of a violent reality?

The answer is a gift to King. Fraser writes:

> In my earliest memory I am an infant lying on my father's bed, being sexually fondled but blissfully unaware of any deception. Then I was treated with tenderness. That was my Garden of Eden.

As in Genesis, pain came with knowledge and expulsion. (1987: 241)

According to Fraser, then, there was a time when she had 'once enjoyed it' (ibid.: 223). Thus King is able to argue:

If repression [proper] does require an 'original' moment of 'turning away' an impulse, then in *My Father's House* this might be represented by Fraser's 'original' moment of *jouissance*, the 'Garden of Eden' where she was 'sexually fondled but blissfully unaware of any deception'. Internal conflicts within the ego, or messages unconsciously picked up from the world outside, might have resulted in the repression of the instinct which sought or responded to this pleasure. (2000: 74)

Here, then, according to King, is the psychoanalytically and properly traumatic event of Fraser's life: the 'real' memory for repression is the Garden of Eden experience. If Fraser had not felt guilty about the pleasure she felt, then she would not have had the mental energy to repress years of abuse, abuse which constantly reminded her of the guilty pleasure she once had; she simply would not have had the wherewithal to hide her father's abuse from herself.

To no uncertain degree, of course, Fraser's narrative works to uphold King's argument. Fraser readily concedes guilty pleasure in the Garden of Eden. But here I want to recall that King performs two readings of Fraser, one might say a split reading. On the one hand, she provides a rigorous and formal reading of the overly constructed, determined nature of *My Father's House* which at every turn works in practice – and despite her caveats – to cast doubt on the plausibility of Fraser's life story. So while King understands that it would be presumptuous to question the truth of her abuse, it is nonetheless 'brought into question by the highly "reconstructed" or novelistic nature of that truth' (ibid.: 68). If read textually, *My Father's House* is just too obvious to ring true. Indeed, at a earlier point in her book, King argues that texts like Fraser's are symptomatic of cultural nostalgia for a time when 'the restoration of lost continuities' was a possibility (ibid.: 29), a time when loss and separation were not known as a reality: a 'pre-Oedipal as Golden Age' (ibid., citing Laura Mulvey). Accordingly, King argues that even narratives like Fraser's

demonstrate the need to find such a memory 'before' the memory of
pain: [Fraser's] evocation of early bliss and innocence demonstrates
the way in which individual psychic and collective cultural myths
mutually reinforce each other: they are so powerful because the pre-
Oedipal is precisely what we *cannot* remember, but what we need to
remember as what has been lost. (ibid.: 28)

According to King, however, this is a cultural trap, since it is
premised 'on the imaginary identification of the pre-Oedipal' (ibid.:
31) and thereby promotes an endless, impossible longing, which represents a refusal to take the journey mapped by Oedipus with the
ensuing complexity and responsibility this brings the subject.

On the other hand, however, King's substantive analysis uses the
Garden of Eden scene to suggest the truth of infantile sexuality.
Thus King deconstructs *My Father's House* and the Garden of Eden
scene to suggest that its truth is culturally governed by regressive
pre-Oedipal nostalgia, while reading it constructively to uphold a
proper, psychoanalytical reading of repression. Formally and sub-
stantively the Garden of Eden scene is used to underwrite the significance of the Oedipal complex. It is real memory when upholding
the significance of the Oedipal complex, and not real if not doing so;
although quite how the Garden of Eden memory becomes symptomatic of a pre-Oedipal desire is a little tricky to guess. At what point
do her memories of abuse figure? Can they figure? Given that the
Garden of Eden memory is the only memory that King affords any
degree of integrity, then my guess is that King was never going to
read Fraser's memoir with reference to anything other than the
importance of the Oedipal myth, and so her use of *Nachträglichkeit*
appears to me to offer little advance on hysteria. So while King cri-
tiques *My Father's House* for being a 'closed system of meaning', the
very same can be said of King's argument. Psychoanalytical readers
can rarely resist, in the end, resorting to a 'correct', correcting
reading, which in this instance means that if Fraser's first and last
memory was the Garden of Eden scene, then the story of Fraser's
trauma was never written for these readers. For King and Showalter,
Fraser's story is an impossible one for her tell. Neither can read any
sign of sexual abuse, which in some perverse, unexpected sense
means that in their desire to place trauma at the service of fantasy

they might yet be reading the impossibility of incest testimony. And while, for obvious reasons, I would not want to press this argument any further, I do want to conclude by saying that we are all ignorant of the trauma inflicted by violence, Fraser included, if her story is to be believed.

CHAPTER 3

Without Insight: Survivor Art and the Possibility of Redemption

Alice Miller is in no doubt that there is a fundamental relationship between the traumas of childhood and creativity. Indeed, according to Miller in her book *The Untouched Key: Tracing Childhood Trauma in Creativity and Destructiveness*, childhood traumas are the 'key' for unlocking the mysteries of art, since their 'traces are always apparent in the person's creative work, usually running through it like a continuous thread' (1990: vii). Taking a visit to a Picasso exhibition as her point of departure, Miller begins her argument by recalling how when walking through the gallery she gradually forgot 'the great crowds of bored people' around her as she is drawn 'inwardly on this adventure. I seemed to be sensing a man's last strenuous efforts to express the most hidden secrets of his life with every means at his disposal before it's too late, before death takes the brush from his hand' (ibid.: 4). Having 'sensed his suffering not only in the themes but also in the force of the brush movements, in the vehement way he sometimes applied colour and conjured up new feelings that had to be given form', Miller forms 'the impression that these paintings express a struggle between what Picasso *must* do and what he is *able* to do, between the necessity of making these strokes and no other, of using this colour and no other' (ibid.). Indeed, Miller senses a desire to 'unlearn the laws of colour theory and composition' for the 'force of necessity increases with such intensity in Picasso's late works that his ability becomes secondary. Feeling is no longer given a shape, as it was in the painting *Guernica*,' she argues; 'now it is lived and becomes pure expression. He no longer does drawing, he no longer counts on the viewer's comprehension; there remains only his haste to produce the unsayable, to say it with colours' (ibid.: 5). Ultimately, then, if somewhat paradoxically, there is a surpassing of art itself in the attempt to say a mysterious 'unsayable' with paint.

Intrigued by and determined to get to the bottom of this mystery, Miller subsequently trawls Picasso's numerous biographies until she discovers that during his childhood his home had been devastated by an earthquake. On the basis of this piece of biography, Miller goes on to correct her earlier understanding of *Guernica* to argue that it 'owes the immediacy of its emotional impact on the viewer' not to Picasso's sense of horror over the bombing of *Guernica* but to 'experiences during the 1884 earthquake in Málaga, experiences that affected his imagination so profoundly that they played an enduring role in his art (ibid.: 12). Although having dismissed *Guernica*, Miller reconsiders its significance in light of her discovery and subsequently argues that it can be understood only in reference to his early childhood trauma which had returned – because of the failing efficiency of his defence mechanisms in old age – to haunt his vision. Thus she concludes 'that his brush was guided by a compulsion he neither understood nor recognised and indeed could not explain because it emerged from his unconscious', and it was only as an old man that he was 'free to paint what his repressed experience dictated' (ibid.: 13). Thus Miller unlocks the mystery of Picasso's art.

There is no question, then, that Miller believes in the residual power of repressed childhood traumas and the redeeming quality of art. Yet her narrative of the relationship between artistic practice and trauma is a troubling one, not least for its romanticism: must the attempt to communicate a traumatically repressed past be cast as an epic struggle? Must it be staged in terms of an almost superhuman effort? Does creativity in the face of trauma have to be so dramatic in scale? And must also the attempt to understand the relationship between trauma and art be cast as mystery requiring special endeavour to solve it? In addition is it necessary to read return of trauma as always already emergent, a force always to be reckoned with and thus always already available for reading, and if so how is this formulation bound to the subjectivity of reading? Simply, do we have to always find great and deep meaning in trauma and art for them both to be significant? While these questions are pertinent enough they have gained considerable significance, given the fact that while Miller might have been obliged to read between the brushstrokes of Picasso's work to discover his trauma, her efforts and thereby her narrative are surely now redundant given the rise of a popular survivor art movement, a movement which ensures that painter and viewer alike fully experience if not also comprehend the images they see. The relationship between pain and paint is now a naked and direct one, or at least certainly it is no longer a question of one man's relationship to his unconsciousness or one woman's experience of strolling through the hallowed space of the modernist gallery. In light of these developments, the aim of this chapter is to produce a less romantic narrative, one that does not require a prior mystery, and one that does rely on the idea that the repressed always leaves a trace and can, if not always will, return to the subject as a matter of intensity.

Miller's reading of *Guernica* is somewhat galling, not only because she reduces its deliberate aesthetic to a question of pure expression, thus running roughshod over his aesthetic attempt to represent the catastrophe at *Guernica*; as Ana Douglass and Thomas Vogler argue, Picasso had uniquely developed a 'semiotic of atrocity' (Douglass and Vogler 2003: 33). Indeed, here it is also interesting to note how at odds Miller's reading is with that of Douglass and Vogler, who argue that:

> The power of artistic 'witness' in [*Guernica*] is not due to Picasso's Spanish blood (i.e., authenticating a legitimate connection to the victims) or to a literal representation of the events. Rather, it is the disruption of conventional modes of representation – the visual rhetoric of rupture. [. . .] One of the century's most familiar icons, it literally turned the stuff of newspapers into art, transforming it from a historical to a symbolic event. (ibid.: 33)

Miller's reading is the very antithesis of this analysis whereupon aesthetic considerations are replaced by history, and the collective, mediated history of a war is ascribed less significance than an apparently transparent and individual psychic injury, and it is this transcription of private for public violence which for many critics is symptomatic of the political limits of the popular turn to trauma.

Among those keen to critique the equation of transparency and personal pain is Roger Luckhurst. Indeed, according to Luckhurst in his article 'Traumaculture', the popularity of recovering traumatic memories does not represent the triumph of creativity over adversity or else provide a means for articulating deep pain, but rather the triumph of a set of historically specific discourses linked to the imperatives of 'the advanced capitalist economies of the West' that have 'locked [into place] a powerful account of selfhood' (2003: 28), one which is based on 'that which *escapes* the subject, on an absence or a gap' (ibid.). Thereby a necessity is created to fill the gap with memories; to make good the 'ominous omissions' (ibid.). By way of a ready-made explanation, trauma can be grasped as a way of filling in the absences, an argument that provides a reworking of the one made by Ian Hacking when he argues that there is 'no canonical way to think of our past. In the endless quest for order and structure, we grasp whatever picture is floating by and put our past into its frame' (1995: 89). Today, the picture we are most likely to grab, it seems, is a traumatic one. According to Luckhurst, then, 'the allure of the recovered memory account and its wider cultural currency is plain to see. In the interstices of a life the loose stitching of mundane details can be unpicked to reveal extraordinary new contents', whereby the

> revelation of traumatic origin offers a singular causation for patterns of life behaviour, for the sense of disappointment or frustration, and a means to re-narrativise the self at a stroke with a new transparency and plenitude generated in a wholly affirmative community. (2003: 32–3)

In addition, however, to producing a certain 'new kind of articulation of subjectivity', Luckhurst draws on the work of Mark Seltzer (1998) to argue that '1990s traumaculture is not only determinable by a set of objects specific to this formation, but is also marked by processes of subjective and communal identification with or projection into the typography of the traumatic gap' (2003: 28). Trauma, it is being argued by both critics, has personal and collective 'allure', which does not simply function to affirm the pain of others. Indeed, for Seltzer, not only is there 'a public fascination with torn and open bodies and torn and opened persons', but 'the very notion of sociality is bound to the excitations of the torn and opened body' (1998: 253). Thus according to both critics the spectacle of trauma stands at the very centre of social and commercial life, whereupon personal and collective identity as well as the imperatives of capital are caught up in the drama of seeing pain. For Luckhurst and a host of other critics, we are drawn in late modernity to dwell upon the scene of violence, whether in memory or in life around us; indeed, the very possibility of society appears now to turn on the spectacle of trauma and thus there is a deep desire to return repeatedly to the site of violence. There is, thus, a compulsion to look that is not our own nor strictly pedagogical: contrary to Miller's experiences of being surrounded by a bored crowd and being the only one drawn on an inward adventure, we are all excited by the prospect of looking at expressions of pain. We all want to insert ourselves into the frame.

Illustrating his argument that profit and something like a prurient interest are mediating the translation of pain into paint, Luckhurst maintains that the success of an artist such as Tracey Emin is due to the fact that her 'work famously mines a traumatic childhood [. . .] (sexual humiliation, rape, and abortion)' (2003: 40), and not due to any aesthetic value her work might have for us. Indeed, he is quick to point out that while the 'instant transparency and controversial contents of [Emin's] work made for rapid success', this was only the case when it had 'crossed the threshold of gallery space and private ownership' when Charles Saatchi bought her most notorious piece of the work, *The Bed*. It seems, then, that Emin and her fans alike have been seduced, if not (unconsciously) compelled, into mistaking the demands and inscriptions of a historically and economically powerful formation for the artist and her art, and thus it might be said that our interest in Emin's work will be passing (so we should not expect it to sustain critical interest like *Guernica*, for example). Or, rather, our interest in Emin's work should be passing, for what appears to concern Luckhurst more than anything is that critics, including academics, are unwilling to develop a suitably analytical language for appraising art such as Emin's and interrogate the 'unproblematised documentary truth claims' made for her confessional aesthetic (ibid.: 41). Thus, according to Luckhurst, 'the wounded narcissism being worked over [by her] art' is passing without conceptual commentary (ibid.: 40). Consequently for Luckhurst the 'critical languages that might abstract this individualised experience have been largely abandoned' (ibid.: 39), and because 'traumatised identities [have] become privileged sites of communality' for everyone, including critics, they need to be compulsively re-staged because there are no longer any theoretical means to process trauma. Trauma is simply presented, over and over, with a seriality that implies, for Freud at least, melancholic entrapment. Compulsively, the shock is renewed but without any advance in comprehension. (ibid.: 39)

There is a constant academic screening of trauma but there is no understanding – or, more pointedly, interrogation – of the image, or the attached subjectivity (ibid.: 42). Thereby it becomes not only necessary but inevitable that Emin will endlessly perform her traumatic identity for us: thus she must invest in the vision of (herself as) a hopelessly melancholic self, a persona forever and forlornly acting out its traumatic history. To this end, then, Luckhurst concludes that Emin's 'success [. . .] seems now strictly circumscribed to the reiterative performance of a trauma through a persona constructed to be constitutively incapable of mastering its own compulsive repetitions' (ibid.: 40–1). Put very bluntly, 'we' require Emin to continually adopt and perform a wounded identity for us: to repeatedly act her pain out for us so we can watch in what might be mock or mild horror.

In sharp contrast to his assessment of (the artwork of) Emin, Luckhurst applauds the serio–comedic work of Tracey Moffatt, work that began in 1994 with *Scarred for Life*, a photographic series of 'ten panels of captioned images that froze in place a moment of psychic damage' (2003: 42) which are based on true stories collected by the artist. Of this work, which includes the image of a naked man in a bedroom lunging after a young girl as she attempts to run from his grasp, he argues that while the images appear to 'recover and fix down the traumatic origin on which a life narrative will subsequently hinge', nonetheless the caption accompanying the image works to undercut the image (in this instance the image caption reads: 'Heart Attack, 1970, She glimpsed him belting the girl from down the street. The day he died of a heart attack'). Luckhurst writes: 'I would tend to see the captioning of these images [. . .] as a comment on the brutal way traumaculture fixes identity through the singular childhood event, destining the self to reiterate this definitional moment without prospect of resolution' (ibid.: 42). According to Luckhurst, however, it is Moffatt's second and distinctly surreal

set of images – *Scarred for Life II* – that works to pass a more definitive political commentary on traumaculture, since the images are
clearly staged reconstructions of trauma. Thereby Luckhurst argues
that: 'The care of the re-staging does not authenticate; rather, it
exaggerates *falsification*. In so doing, the series plays with but also
exposes the allure of the impossible recovery of original plenitude
that is at the heart of traumaculture' (ibid.: 43).

In counterpoint to his assessment of Emin's work, Luckhurst is
keen to uphold Moffatt's work, for while it clearly solicits an interest
in the representation of trauma it is also understood by Luckhurst to
undercut that interest and turn it back on the viewer. Our interest in
the image is not unqualified; our desire to adopt the image is queried
by the 'archness' of design and 'studiedly neutral language of the
captions' (2003: 43). Here, Luckhurst considers Moffatt's work
important because it offers an interrogation of the promises and pleasures that he sees underpinning the work of Emin and traumaculture
per se. According to Luckhurst, then, it is impossible to place oneself
– whether as a viewer or victim of trauma – in a surrealist image
without questioning why one is looking in the first place; hence, identification is thwarted by the deliberate artifice of the image; it is not
possible to be simply absorbed in and by the image.

In contrast Emin's work does not make us stop and think as such.
It is all laid bare for us. Thus for Luckhurst, Emin's habit of publicly
airing the dirty laundry of her life, as she does quite literally with *The
Bed*, trades on the illusion that her unmade bed equals an unmade
truth, hence we do not have to 'think' on it; critically, then, for
Luckhurst, we are left 'sleeping on it'. But as Luckhurst's use of the
neologism 'traumaculture' suggests, artists such as Emin appear to
have forgotten that there is a creative interval between reality and representation, a gap which because it has to be actively traversed by the
viewer is for him the space of political commentary, and because it is
negotiated in the moment of looking works against passive viewing.

In some respects, Luckhurst's desire to critique the turn to
trauma is laudable and serves as a welcome check on the romanticism of Miller's reading and her desire to reduce art to the affects of
personal history. The idea that art can show us things as they really
were and can thus put us in the picture is one the founding deceits
of realism, and a critical attitude to the illusions held fast by this

aesthetic is a political necessity. Moreover, Luckhurst's emphasis on the necessity for a de-individuating analysis and an analysis cautioning against the desire for plenitude in affect and meaning is highly useful, and I share many of his concerns. On all counts, Miller can be held to account; indeed, her narrative of sublime inspiration and her desire to install childhood trauma as the origin of art is deeply troubling, since it risks reproducing a redeeming logic. Despite the cynically critical cast of his reading, I am not, however, convinced that Luckhurst's narrative differs that greatly from Miller's. For, crucially, he finds inspiration in Moffatt's work and in this sense he is no different from Miller, since in effect they both measure the value of art by its capacity to promote intellectual interest, to provoke their thought, to be an occasion for thinking. They both want a key to unlock the meaning of art: for Miller the key is childhood trauma, whereas for Luckhurst the key is aesthetic design. Thus Luckhurst dismisses Emin and her art because it does not engender (his) critical thought, whereas Moffatt's work gives Luckhurst the perfect return on (his) interest: it prompts instant thinking. Perversely it might yet be the case that at least in terms of knowledge production, Moffatt's image is servicing a capitalist understanding of knowledge, whereas Emin's work does not, in that it actually gives very little in return; it is a poor investment. If this is the case, could it not be read as an aesthetic that seeks to rein in the critic's visual appetite? Or as an aesthetic that tells us that truth will disappoint us or as an aesthetic that tells us how easily truth can be lost if it does not and cannot live up to our expectations? Or as an aesthetic telling us of a poor truth with little possibility of offering the viewer a sense of enlightenment?

What Luckhurst and Miller share, then, is a desire for a greater truth, a more satisfying truth. They seek it differently and in different places, to be sure, but in the end they both seek a truth capable of sustaining their desire. Of course, Luckhurst readily admits that he is looking for a critical aesthetic, but I would want to suggest that he is a little quick to judge the value of the art he dislikes and thereby misses an opportunity to rethink its political significance. For you do not have to be a fan of Emin's work to argue that the challenge presented by it and trauma art more generally is whether, politically speaking, it is necessary to make a sustaining meaning out of it. Is it possible then to read trauma art without freighting it with our expectations for what can count as a political comment? Without reading undo significance into it? Without expecting it to give us something in return for our interest? A way of reading that does not labour the truth or else seek reward in truth? Might Emin not say, 'I have shown you everything and you want more from me'?

Given that Miller is cited as an influence and given that it is dated to the 1990s, it is not surprising that *She Who Is Lost Is Remembered: Healing from Incest Through Creativity* (Wisechild 1991) – an anthology of incest art, poetry and creative writing – is based on a belief in the power of art to represent previously hidden and occluded traumas that would otherwise remain concealed from view. Indeed, there is repeated reference to the idea that art is perhaps the sole medium for envisioning the inner horrors of family life. Rehearsing the idea that art can reveal the unseen side of domestic and psychic life, Kim Newall notes, for example, that her 'pictures tell the secrets' that she had concealed from herself and her family (1991: 2), while Katherine F. H. Heart attests to the fact that painting helps her 'to capture raw feelings as they emerge from unconscious to conscious awareness' and in so doing allow her to discover aspects of her abuse that she had not previously known (1991: 152). Typical in this respect is Bonnie Martinez, who considers art to be a particularly powerful, if not privileged, medium for 'exploring and expurgating the memories' of abuse, even when they have been repressed for decades, as they had been for her. As a process of enabling the direct visualisation and expression of memories, art is thus understood by Martinez to have been 'a means for my subconscious to try to make contact with my conscious mind and feelings' (1991: 122).

Indeed, for Martinez this process of painting her way through her pain was so potent that she began to see the past quite differently, as she writes:

A curious thing about the memories was that as I was actually seeing what was happening to me, and thinking about it later, I came to realise that the visual images had more actual clarity than I am capable of at my present age. At first, I couldn't figure it out. Then I realized that I was 'seeing' what happened to me with the eyes of a child – undimmed by the time and the need to not see. (ibid.: 124)

Illustrative of Martinez's new and miraculous insight is *Father as Fetish Figure, or Din, Din for Baby*, a large oil painting of a baby quietly terrorised as it has a disembodied penis shoved into its yawning mouth. With little in the way of background detail, it is an image that fills the frame, organising without equivocation its visual significance: there is precious little to see but a distressed baby being subjected to oral rape. Via what is taken to be the extraordinary mimetism of art and because her powers of repression are waning, Martinez gets to eventually see, here, what happened to her for the very first time. By placing – and seeing – herself in this image, which is understood by her to be representative, Martinez is finally able to speak of that which was, at the time, quite literally unspeakable and thereby achieve a sense of resolution. 'In that sense', she concludes, 'it has been a wonderful experience of clarity. It doesn't make up for what has happened in any way, but it has offered me a moment of beauty among all the ugliness' (ibid.). There is no doubt here, then, that Martinez believes in the power of art to redeem the past by giving her vision of it. Or, indeed, more precisely, she believes art restores insight by returning her to the point in history when repression became a necessity. In the strongest possible sense, art does not simply allow Martinez to 'put the memory down visually' (ibid.: 122), but it works to put her down in the scene, with her capacity to register what was happening fully restored.

The idea that art can place the artist *and* the spectator back at the scene is, for Martinez, the redemptory promise of realism – its unmediated access allows for the truth to be seen by all: we all get (to be in) the picture. Indeed, key to Martinez's ideas about the role of art in her recovery, and somewhat paradoxically, is how little art plays a role: so, for example, during this period she stresses how the compulsion to free herself of 'the agony of the experience' served to drive, dominate and eventually eclipse aesthetic concerns. Thus Martinez concedes that the paintings from this period were the largest she had ever done, for it was 'as if the need to encompass the enormity of the experiences demanded as much space as I was capable of handling', and 'all the love of painting for the joy of it – for the color, the texture – became secondary. The obsession was freeing myself of the images that were haunting me' (ibid.: 124). Ultimately, then, painting was not an aesthetic process, it was 'documentary'. It was, she writes, a matter of producing 'Concrete visualization. Solid visual, irrefutable screaming proof of the incest. No more silence. Clear pictures for everyone to see. No doubt about it having happened' (ibid.: 122). In a sense, then, the art is bracketed as history is revealed to her and to us. The art counts for little, it is what we see and not how we see that counts, and what we see are the ugly scenes of childhood restored to plain sight. There is no artifice at play here for Martinez, and none is meant to be at play for us either.

The idea that there is nothing at play here except the revelation of a horrific yet previously unknown reality has, as I noted above, met with deep scepticism. But while it would be easy to expose the illusion that *Father as Fetish Figure* provides an unmediated access to the past, it is important to stall this critique in order to ask whether or not Martinez's art has something else to say to us other than what she or, indeed, Luckhurst, might intend it to say. Whatever else it might be, this is a shocking image, and one I feel that is not so easily read as symptomatic of the power of discourse or else bracketed from consideration (as Luckhurst quite literally does when making reference to the traumatic events of Emin's life). By stuffing the image of a life-size penis into the image of an equally life-size baby there is a straining of the visual field: it is difficult to accommodate the two images within the same frame. The introduction of the penis into the baby's mouth forces a radical split between the reality of one person's childhood and the ideal image of childhood. Despite the transcendent illusions that underpin it, this image is not meant to be a larger than life representation, but more simply an image conveying a truth, the enormity of which is hard to grasp. For as the painting title suggests there is a fundamental impasse separating the language of violence literally sustaining the silence of the child ('din, din for baby') and the language symbolically sustaining the romance of family life ('father as a fetish figure'). The baby is meant to swallow the myth not the reality; indeed, here she does not know it as a myth, having been made instead to live it as reality. She has no idea what is happening and no way of formulating a language for herself, thus she is literally and symbolically speechless. Her life is 'spoken for' by the desires of another: 'din, din for baby'. Indeed, the idea that the imposition of desire is food for development is a savage projection of the fact that the act of violence is a way of nourishing the desires of the father; it is, of course, the baby who functions as a fetish for the projecting and violating desires of her father. Indeed, given the fact that *Father as Fetish Figure* is based on a memory recovered from when Martinez was eighteen months old, the age when psychoanalytically speaking the child is understood to enter language and is thereby at the onset of creative and conceptual development, Martinez is forcibly gagged at this stage and her development is stopped dead in its tracks; thus she is unable to take the imaginative leap from silence to speech and other forms of symbolic expression. As a consequence, she has no means of representing to herself, let alone others, what is happening to her, and thereby it can have no meaning for her. It is little surprise, then, that she forgot; she forgot because she was not capable of remembering in the first place, unable to start the process of creating a world for herself, until picking up a paintbrush as an adult.

But is a paintbrush enough to handle the enormity of violence? Despite Martinez's confidence, the image can be read as demonstrating the limits of her attempt to handle the 'enormity of [her] experiences'. Symbolically, at least, if Martinez is seeing her abuse through this image, she cannot bring herself to see (herself seeing) this scene, since the baby's eyes are represented by black holes which are themselves partially shut by the force of the abuse. The baby is lost for vision. Strictly speaking, then, if *Father as Fetish Figure* is meant to represent the clarity gained through 'seeing what happened [. . .] with the eyes of a child – undimmed by time and the need to not see' it can only give the lie to that possibility. Hence, the eyes remain unseeing, unable to contemplate the scene. Martinez can place herself at the scene but only, it seems, at the cost of a repeating blindness. In the final analysis, *Father as Fetish Figure* is an image that does not proffer the insight it imagines for itself, and thus it can be read as representing the impossibility, not the possibility, of beholding the scene of incest. The tyranny of the event is acted out and replicated at the level of representation: violence, one might argue here, is not food for thought, and nor is 'Think on this' the condition of possibility for creative thinking but rather its violent end, leaving precious little to see.

I am not, of course, the only feminist critic keen to seek a less redemptive aesthetic for the representation of incest; this possibility is also explored by Janet Marstine in her recent article on the incest survivor and artist Jane Orleman. Inspired by a recognition of the limits of realist representations, Marstine maintains that incest 'defies synthesis and transcendence' (which are the very cornerstones of realism and representation), and thus art cannot resolve the horror of trauma; or, more precisely, mimesis cannot redeem the radically evasive reality of trauma by reconciling the viewer with its image (2002: 633). Acknowledging the import of Theodor W. Adorno's oft-cited and widely debated maxim that 'to write poetry after Auschwitz is barbaric', Marstine seeks to query the pleasures afforded by realism and demands instead for 'the transformation of art from the harmonic and knowable to the jarring and irresolvable' (ibid.). In pursuit of what I shall call an anti-redemptive aesthetic, Marstine essentially commits herself to the belief that there is never and there cannot ever be a complete(d) vision of trauma, since to imagine or do otherwise would amount to a political and ethical denial of what is essentially traumatic about incest: namely its affront to personal and collective understanding. Politically and ethically it is a matter of preserving the power of this affront, since this alone will ensure a perpetual provocation, working against the desire to settle the account of trauma.

Uniquely, however, Marstine exploits the increasingly familiar idea that art cannot redeem atrocity and that mimesis will inevitably fail to represent it to counteract a long-standing repudiation of art therapy. Animated by the idea that it is impossible to symbolically integrate and render immanent traumatic experiences, Marstine argues that 'representations of trauma would not simply exist as art without also referencing the therapeutic struggle' (ibid.: 633). This is a politically significant move that not only renders secular some of the distinctly sacral readings of Adorno, but also connects the debates generated by Adorno's pronouncement to the personal testimony politics informing the production of incest art. In making this connection, Marstine opens up the possibility of advancing personal testimony politics without relying on a naive realism and without turning to anti-realism (which invariably foregrounds and privileges issues of representation over a concern with the referent – however nominally this might be interpreted); more specifically, she offers a way of reading the limits of realism as politically productive. To this end, her argument requires a somewhat attentive reading. However, it also warrants this attention because I also think that Marstine fails in her task, and as a result there is a missed opportunity to demonstrate precisely why an anti-redemptive aesthetic lends itself to a feminist reading of incest representation.

To demonstrate what art looks like if it references the struggle to represent trauma, Marstine offers a close analysis of the work of Orleman, who, it is important to note, depicts her experiences of sexual and physical abuse in 'painstaking detail' (ibid.: 634). According to Marstine, then, *My First Memory* is typical of Orleman's ability to convey the horrific nature of her experiences. Marstine describes the picture as follows:

> Here is a doll house gone awry. The decorative china plates, the yellow flowers on the table, and the old-fashioned screen door, which allows a glimpse of the verdant rural landscape, evoke feelings of nostalgia, only to be interrupted by the horror of the act of molestation, a tiny diaper thrown carelessly on the floor, and of isolation, as a child-witness turns her back to the scene, unwilling or unable to respond. The three-year-old victim lying on the dining table glazes over and turns inward as the family 'friend' masturbates while touching her until she is raw. (ibid.)

Depicting the perpetrator visibly masturbating while penetrating the child with his finger, Orleman represents the scene of abuse in graphic and shocking detail. But in counterpoint to the shock provoked by *Father as Fetish Figure*, Marstine argues that *My First Memory* 'shows the power of mimesis' by demonstrating its inadequacy. In what is a quite significant departure from the type of reading normally solicited by realist representations of incest, Marstine argues that 'No matter how closely the painting captures the terror of the moment, the past is elusive. Through mimesis, Orleman leads the viewer to understand that representation is a pale reflection of the pain of sexual trauma' (ibid.). Unlike the mimetic fidelity explicitly assumed by the artwork of Martinez, *My First Memory* is understood by Marstine to reveal that mimesis is no match for the reality of incest. Thus even if it were possible to mirror the scene of incest detail for detail, it would still not be enough to convey that reality.

Developing her reading of Orleman's anti-redemptive aesthetic, Marstine maintains that Orleman does not offer confessional images since these would merely declare themselves as the truth by pinpointing the truth in the manner of *Father as Fetish Figure*. Indeed, as counterintuitive and provocative as it sounds, confessional images are 'easy on the eye' to the extent that they demand nothing from the viewer – essentially they perform themselves, or rather they require so little from the viewer that they appear to do so. *Father as Fetish Figure* is rhetorical in this sense, since it assumes that it has no need for the viewer to demonstrate 'its' truth. Hence, typically, realism dispenses with the viewer – or rather it is the classic ruse of realism to appear to dispense with the viewer. In reality, or at least ideologically, the viewer is so completely in accord with the expectations of the image that they are – seamlessly and without knowing or effort – part of its meta-framework. There is simply a correspondence on and of the relationship between reality, image and viewer. Alternatively Marstine argues that Orleman offers the viewer testimonial images – images that question the constitution or production of their truth (and hence viewing subjectivity), not tell or otherwise scream it. Here, the work of a testimonial image is not complete because it requires the active engagement of the viewer: it is, indeed, waiting for an answer. This said, however, how does *My First Memory* differ from *Father as Fetish Figure*?

In an attempt to formally distinguish the testimonial quality of Orleman's images, Marstine makes a number of claims about Orleman's aesthetic practice. First, she notes that Orleman 'creates the voice of the testimonial by consciously using a childlike technique', which in turn 'enables her to access the insights of her girlhood and to disrupt the viewer from the voyeuristic pleasure of objectification' (ibid.: 639). Second, Marstine argues that Orleman 'combine[s] the childlike technique with a narrative quasi-documentary approach to evoke the tension of mimesis' (ibid.).

Leaving aside the question of how or why adopting a childlike voice provides access to childhood memories (other than through a straightforward faith in mimesis), and certainly putting aside her untenable claim that a childlike technique blocks voyeuristic interest, it is at this point that Marstine's argument starts to break down, when she notes that Orleman frequently combines the childlike and quasi-documentary techniques by 'working on a miniature scale reminiscent of Renaissance altarpiece *predella* panels', and 'although her attention to story-telling makes the images seem fetishistic, the paintings, when seen as a group, create a metanarrative of gender and power' (ibid.). Having already noted her use of the quasi-documentary, and having conceded that Orleman's predilection for miniature detail might be seen as fetishistic – if it were not viewed through the meta-lens of power and gender – Marstine de facto attributes to Orleman's work a readily evidenced symbolic power, and thereby it is hard to discover how Orleman's painting 'leads the viewer to understand that representation is a pale reflection of the pain of sexual trauma'.

In a bid to shore up her argument, Marstine subsequently deploys the concept of traumatic realism to maintain that Orleman's images are testimonial; in other words they require the viewer to complete them. Taking her lead from Michael Rothberg's (2000) use of the concept, Marstine argues that traumatic realism forces the viewer to question their relationship to post-traumatic culture precisely because there is a juxtaposing of the extreme and the everyday which, since it establishes a visual tension, 'reflects the impossibility of integrating them into understanding' (2002: 634). To this end, Marstine argues that Orleman's images acquire their power because they highlight 'the irreconcilable disjunction between the small voice of the child and the cataclysmic events against which she is powerless' (ibid.). Demonstrating, finally, how the traumatic realism of Orleman's images work in practice, Marstine argues that Orleman's *Deep Dark Secret*

> elicits in us feelings of comfort only to arrest them with the horror of the atrocities committed. The image of the child, chained naked in a coal cellar, is made more shocking by the quotidian environment in the living room above and by glimpses of a pleasant landscape

beyond. Details on the main floor such as a white doily on an arm-chair and a man's hat hanging from a mirror overwhelm us with their ordinary nature. These details force us to ask ourselves how abuse may have invaded our own seemingly ordinary lives and the life of our community. (ibid.: 639)

It is at this point, however, that Marstine's anti-redemptive argument finally collapses. To begin with, Marstine argues that the power of Orleman's images lies in the fact that they question the viewer (which is to say that they cannot and do not completely organise the visual field for the viewer). But judging by Marstine's reading, *My First Memory* and *Deep Dark Secret* provide the answers to any questions they might pose. Put simply, the viewer does not have to look any further than these images to know the truth of incest since these pictures alone provide a complete, if painstaking, vision. The problem with Marstine's application of traumatic realism and her attempt to forge a politically informed anti-redemptive aesthetic is that she makes the details of the image do the work of truth-telling, despite acknowledging that the trauma of incest cannot be captured by the mimetic powers of realism. Indeed, in what I take to be her attempt to do justice to the images, Marstine's own reading is itself painstaking in its detail. Marstine fetishes the details of the images as indices of truth that if read cumulatively will express the larger picture. They are meant as concrete details that secure the visual significance of the image; they act as points of reference. Thus the detail serves as the referent of the visual field in precisely the same way that the penis is meant to organise the visual significance of *Father as Fetish Figure*. Indeed, like Martinez, Orleman repeatedly relies on the shock provoked by showing it all in its explicit detail. Without realising it, Marstine reinvests the detail (such as the nappy) with a transcendent and synthesising power; likewise Martinez and Orleman (re)invest the penis with the same power. Put differently, the details – including the visibly present penis – are understood to mediate a relationship between the real and the symbolic, and in so doing they figure a traumatic truth where, in fact, as Marstine has attested, trauma cannot be attributed a symbolic or metaphorical value. No matter how empirically 'accurate' the representation, it does not mirror the reality. The details are shocking, but they are details that alone do not establish or guarantee solid meaning. As Griselda Pollock argues, trauma 'cannot be collapsed into empirical anatomy – visible fact' (2001: 116). The truth of trauma cannot be extrapolated from empirical details; they do not furnish us with the meaning of violence.

Acknowledging that it might not be possible to image the truth by simply attaching a politically symbolic weight to the detail is key to the work of Linda Ness, who is the only artist contributing to *She Who Is Lost Is Remembered* who can be read as self-consciously querying the promise of realism to provide a window on the reality of incest. To this end, *Bible Reading* (Figure 1) – a brightly coloured acrylic painting depicting a father and his daughters praying at a dinner table, while another daughter stands by him reading the bible – is an exception among the images in the anthology. What distinguishes *Bible Reading* is that it serves as a shocking representation of incest *and* as a commentary on the ability of the viewer to see the details of the scene. Here, the shock of this image is not placed centre frame for all to immediately see (as it is in Martinez's *Father as Fetish Figure*) but is held in the bottom of the image, particularly in the left-hand corner, where it takes a moment or two before its significance is taken in. However, because the eye is formally swept away from the detail of abuse, it is, in fact, difficult for the viewer not to find that they are outside and beyond the scene of incest. But, unlike Orleman's images there is no content to this outside beyond, and hence it does not serve as a context or contrast by which to illuminate the significance of the interior; it is an unenlightening darkness. In other words, the darkness does not symbolise anything, contrary also to the black holes of *Father as Fetish Figure* (which are meant to represent the depths of trauma). In keeping with Marstine's original insight, trauma evades symbolic representation. There is no way of seeing in darkness/or what is in darkness. Structurally, then, this image queries whether it is possible for the symbolic to contain the trauma of incest (and the interest of the viewer).

The fact that the viewer of the image finds that they are outside and beyond the realm of representation is significant for two, interrelated, reasons. First, there is a visual delay at work that means that the viewer does not experience an instant return when looking at the image. *Father as Fetish Figure* is explicitly premised on the idea that

Figure 1 Bible Reading, 1990, 22" x 24", acrylic on canvas.

the viewer will immediately absorb, almost without knowing, the significance of the image; hence the viewer is afforded instant, if blind-
ing, access to the horror it depicts. Indeed, it is predicated on the
belief that the viewer cannot fail to take it in: you are looking directly
at it and in 'return' you will also achieve a stunning insight. To this

end, *Father as Fetish Figure* promises Martinez *and* the viewer the 'beauty of seeing'; here, seeing the truth is rendered a (seductively) sublime experience. Although, given that the viewer already knows how to read it and what to expect from it, they have, in a sense, already seen it; they have seen it all before. The rhetoric of realism always carries the possibility of boredom, which is why there is a constant search for something really sublime.

Bible Reading, however, queries this investment in seeing by offering *and* denying this satisfaction or return on our interest. The attention of the viewer is drawn away, interrupted if not terminally delayed by the studiously blank window. This works to structurally offset – or at least complicate – the desire of the viewer to imagine that they can easily contemplate the image. *Bible Reading* thus cautions against the promise of an instant, interior (if perhaps bottomless, sublime) view. Of course, there is a risk here that the viewer's satisfaction is simply heightened by the labour of seeing, but this would be to deny the extent to which the viewer's attention is being constantly directed to a point beyond the abuse. The point of fascination is the window not the abuse, and the window itself says little. The window does not provide a point of entry or insight, but likewise it does not allow the viewer to escape. In sum, the viewer is kept within the scene but without any pay-off.

A second and related point is that there is also a sense in which there is no access for the victim either. Indeed, symbolically, none of the daughters, including the daughter standing by his side, see the abuse, but rather they are depicted with their eyes shut or otherwise distracted by the acts of praying and reading. Their blindness is underscored, moreover, by the fact that the actions of the father are hidden from their view by virtue of the domesticity of the scene (represented by the table); the trappings of femininity (represented by the skirt); and by his law (provocatively represented here by the Bible). Here, then, the trauma itself destroys vision, producing, as Dori Laub (1995) has argued, 'an event without a witness'. No one has or possesses the inside view, perhaps least of all the victims, since they cannot bear to witness the horror of what is happening to them. This reading is confirmed by another of Ness's images, *Out of Body*, an aerial view of a child's bedroom where a distraught anthropomorphic 'object' lies on the bed in an otherwise empty room.

According to Ness this picture represents the fact that when she was being abused by her father she learnt to leave her traumatised body, whereupon she would view the abuse from 'the corner of the ceiling' – which is to say from a perspective beyond herself. Once again, the viewer's visual interest is drawn away from the scene of violation to the window of the room, although this time the viewer is attracted by the visual energy of curtains blowing wildly in a window that is thrown open to the elements. This shift to the window, however, works structurally (rather than symbolically) to ally the viewer with the position assumed by the trauma victim as she views herself from the ceiling corner, and thus opens the possibility of a mutual view, if not indicating the mutuality of any view.

Out of Body suggests, then, that the survivor and viewer are always forced to view the trauma of incest from beyond – or from a point outside of – the 'literal' details of abuse. Put differently, truth is not understood to simply reside in the body or at the scene of abuse, whereupon truth becomes a function of either returning to the interior, or conversely a matter of exorcising inner demons; nor is truth figured as beyond reach as a radical exteriority (since both of these are mutually constitutive conceits), but rather this is to suggest an economy of truth or reality that operates at the limits of this onto-logical design. What is significant, then, about the window (of viewing) in *Out of Body* is that it establishes the point of perspec-tive at 'the very threshold of a visibility that is borderline of what we can bear to watch' (Pollock 2001: 153). Insight can only be found at the borderline of inside and outside, visibility and invisibility, and most importantly at the point where victim (self) and viewer (other) meet, so that 'Art may lead us to discover our part of the shared responsibility in the events that are not "inside" the Other-self' (Bracha Lichtenberg Ettinger, cited in ibid.: 144–5). Importantly, though, this is not the sharing of a pious responsibility, for, as *Bible Reading* emphatically asserts, a pious respect for the law is itself implicated in the reproduction of trauma: a certain blasphemy and disrespect is the order of the day. To this end, the not–quite–void left by trauma cannot function as a sublime experience or the unfath-omability of another's trauma. Reaching for the depths of horror and breaching the impasse is a necessary transgression, precisely because 'none of this is emptiness; it is not-yet signified, or rather, it hovers at the limits of signification awaiting some filter for its affects to traverse that threshold without ever being able to be contained with existing signs' (ibid.: 116). If, as Pollock argues, trauma is waiting for an aesthetic to translate its significance without capturing it, how might we understand this possibility?

This is the question that preoccupies Jill Bennett in her *Empathic Vision: Affect, Trauma, and Contemporary Art*. With an eye to the critique of popular trauma culture and taking her lead from Gilles Deleuze, Bennett is looking to advance a trauma aesthetic that does not aim to 'reproduce the world (the Renaissance conception of art as representation)', but rather aims to register and produce affect: 'affect, not as opposed to or distinct from thought, but as the means by which a kind of understanding is produced' (2005: 32). Crucially Bennett is looking for a type of art that 'touches us, but does not necessarily communicate the "secret" of personal experience' (ibid.), and has the power to move the viewer but doing so 'not in the sense that narrative engenders an empathic response through identification with characters, but in the more literal sense of inciting affect' (ibid.). – critically, an affect that 'does not equate with emotion or sympathy', and nor 'does it necessarily attach to persons or to characters in the first instance' (ibid.: 9–10). Thus she is arguing for a move away from the traps of 'crude empathy' – a 'feeling for another based on the assimilation of the other's experience to the self' – toward an art that exploits 'forms of embodied perception in order to promote forms of critical inquiry' (ibid.: 10). 'This conjunction of affect and critical awareness may be understood', she argues, 'to constitute the basis of an empathy grounded not in affinity (feeling for another insofar as we can imagine being that other) but on a feeling for another that entails an encounter with something irreducible and different, often inaccessible' (ibid.).

Importantly, then, Bennett is looking for art that presents a check on empathetic identification – which all too readily reproduces the schema of good and evil that she finds typical of popular culture. In other words, she is looking for art that does not 'foreclose on the possibility of elaborating a description of traumatic experience that addresses the moral ambiguities of lived experience' (ibid.: 27). In an effort to illustrate what is at stake with an art practice that suspends moral judgement, Bennett looks to the representation of child sexual abuse. According to Bennett, and she is not wrong, such abuse is typically figured in rather stark moral terms, and certainly this is the case with most of the artworks featuring in *She Who Is Lost Is Remembered*. As a result Bennett argues that this leaves

> little space for exploring the subjective experience of either perpetrator or survivor, both of whom frequently confound moral categorisation. How can a survivor describe the experience of rape perpetrated by a loved one – or that of 'becoming sexualised' at an early age – from the perspective of an innocent? (ibid.: 27)

In order to explore these questions she argues that we need 'open artistic inquiry' (ibid.: 28), which means 'not only circumventing classification, however, but moving outside a representational practice that aims to comment on its subject matter' (ibid.). As an example of such art, Bennett explores the 'expansive' work of Dennis Del Favero and his series of ten large photographs *Parting Embrace*. On her reading Bennett argues that the visually opaque images of incoherent mounds of flesh and a visually occluded boy with his mouth yawning open seek 'to register the pain of abuse as physical imprint', and in so doing 'the imagery offers a vision from the body, embracing in the process a certain moral ambiguity' (ibid.). Commenting on how the artist understands his work in terms of 'the pornography and the violence of memories of abuse' and in terms of the not always distinct elements of love and fantasy, Bennett argues that 'the affects of fear, humiliation, shock and so on, may be tied to the same objects as those of joy and excitement' (ibid.). In other words, she argues ' "love" may characterise an aspect of the relationship one has with an abuser – particularly in an incestuous relationship where the victim has an emotional attachment to the abuser, *notwithstanding the pain or trauma that may occupy abuse*' (ibid.). Thereupon she argues that the ten-plate series divides down the middle, with the first five images representing *Parting* and the second set representing *Embrace*. As the title suggests, she argues, the

> second set of images, which are softer, and more diffused, cast memories in a more positive, romantic hues than the more overtly disturbing and hard-core *Parting*. Here, then, the mix of feelings, sensations,

and emotion that characterise the experience of abuse for certain survivors is privileged at the cost of moral clarity. (ibid.: 29)

While I am happy to subscribe to Bennett's demand for 'nonaffirmative forms of art' and for art that does 'not offer a clear political statement in the manner of didactic works' (ibid.: 20, 21), I fail to see how, on her reading, *Parting Embrace* does not pass explicit commentary on the experience, and I certainly see little experimentation here: the idea that only a thin line separates love and hate is commonplace, to say the least; that secretly somewhere deep inside us we can be confused by and possibly enjoy the humiliation inflicted by so-called loved ones is a pedestrian idea, not something that belongs as an idea to critics looking to laud the merits of reputedly experimental art. Indeed, what I see is nothing less than a reworking of a rather tired pornographic narrative: first we have the pain, the 'no', but if we give into or embrace the chaos of emotion, we find we can have pleasure: 'yes'. The idea that 'no' will yield to 'yes' if we are open to its possibility is a well-worn trope, not the mark of avant-garde art. This is not the view from the body, or rather if it is the view from the body, it is body with a full store of ready-to-hand cultural narratives to explain 'the pain or trauma that *may* occupy abuse'. Despite the virtues of her analysis, I find Bennett's effort to establish the power of images in relation to the affect they produce deeply problematic. Indeed, when she argues that the affect produced by Favero's work is 'not organised in terms of emotion or the expression of individual characters', I struggle to see how this is not the case. The characters are simply different from the more conventional figuring of victims and perpetrators maybe, but they are familiar enough characters nonetheless.

While Luckhurst and Bennett look to the formalism of conceptual art to find meaning, and while Miller found it necessary to trawl Picasso's biographies for clues to the meaning of his art, today it is simply a matter of trawling the internet to discover the meaning of trauma. No longer the preserve of Picasso and his complex aesthetic, or the aesthetic of Moffatt or Favero, the practice of trauma art has experienced a veritable explosion, as exemplified by the Survivor Art Gallery of Abuse and Trauma (www.survivorart.com) – a web-based

Figure 2 The Evil One, 2003, 18.8" x 15", mixed media.

'night gallery of trauma' that plays host to 'Survivors of abuse, mental illness, P.O.W. and real life horrors' as they 'speak without words'. Among the artists featured on the website is Regina Lafay. Like all the other artists I have considered, Lafay is a survivor of sexual abuse who finds redemption in her art. She writes: 'Through art, I am able to express myself in ways I cannot put into words. I discover and I heal. And sometimes I just scream. We all need to scream, and art is a quieter, more productive way of doing so.' Her most interesting image is, however, *The Evil One* (Figure 2). What is significant about this image (aside from the fact that it is found via a link to her commercial website), and what makes it so radically different from her other images, as well as the images by Martinez, Ness and Orleman, is its use of pop art, an aesthetic that contradicts the very principles and signatures of trauma art: authenticity; experience; immediacy; presence.

Yet it was in relation to Andy Warhol and pop art that Hal Foster developed his influential account of traumatic realism, a reference overlooked by many critics seeking to mobilise his work, including

Luckhurst and (via Rothberg) Marstine. Indeed, what Luckhurst and Marstine do not appreciate is how traumatic realism was meant as a concept to bridge the tendency of reading images as either simulacral or referential. Thus both fail to understand that the language of traumatic realism is an attempt to read the image as 'referential' (all, presence) and 'simulacral' (nothing, absence), which also means reading the artist as a subject exercising and not exercising control over the aesthetic design and 'meaning' of their work, as a subject with referential depth and subjective interiority, as well as being superficial, impassive. Developing this reading in relation to Warhol's *Death in America* series in particular, Foster argues that the images can be read 'as referential *and* simulacral, connected *and* disconnected, affective *and* affectless, critical *and* complacent' (1995: 130). As a consequence, and key at this point, Foster argues how this simultaneous reading works to alter our understanding of the role and function of 'repetition' in pop art. According to Foster, the repetitions of pop art, whether actual or inferred, are typically understood to drain the image of significance and thus defend against affect. They occupy the visual field by exhausting themselves of authentic meaning or by demonstrating the exhaustion of authentic meaning, and in the process leave little for the viewer to feel or think, or else get attached to. Thus, on one level, as Foster argues, the repetitions of pop art perform the work of mourning where the point is to repeat the traumatic event until it is stripped of affect in order that it can be integrated into the symbolic order; once there – at a remove – it can be understood and thus no longer experienced as traumatic.

Yet Foster also argues 'the Warhol repetitions are not restorative in this way; they are not about a mastery of trauma. More than a patient release from the object in mourning, they suggest an obsessive fixation on the object in melancholy' (ibid.: 131–2). Yet again he continues to argue a reading in terms of melancholy is not right either, since

> Warholian repetitions not only *re*produce traumatic effects, they also *produce* them. Somehow in these repetitions, then, several contradictory things occur at the same time: a warding away of traumatic significance *and* an opening out to it, a defending against traumatic affect *and* a producing of it. (ibid.: 132)

Critically, then, Foster writes

> repetition in Warhol is not reproduction in the sense of representa-
> tion (of a referent) or simulation (of a pure image, or detached signi-
> fier). Rather, repetition serves to *screen* the real understood as
> traumatic. But this very need also points to the real, and at this point
> ruptures the screen of repetition. It is a rupture less in the world than
> in the subject – between the perception and the consciousness of a
> subject *touched* by an image. (ibid.)

Crucially what Foster is arguing here is that the critical force of traumatic art is to be found in the viewing subject who is touched by the
image. Of course, I have problematised the idea of the viewer being
touched or otherwise moved and inspired by the image throughout
this chapter, but I want to argue that Foster is suggesting an economy
of touch that does not prompt critical thought in the manner suggested by Bennett. Indeed, she is quite clear that her analysis is a
'steer away from what has been termed "traumatic realism"'' because
as she understands it, it is based on art that 'assaults us' or else
'thrust[s] us involuntarily into a mode of critical inquiry' (2005: 11),
whereas she is concerned with the 'conjunction of affect and cognition'. This, however, is not my reading of Foster, for, as I understand
it, he is not looking for a critical agency to spring from the violent
rupture of affect and cognition, but rather he is looking for a critical
agency somewhere between them – or, even more precisely, for an
agency springing from the experience of not quite thinking, and not
quite feeling. Indeed, what is striking about Bennett's model is how
easily and fully affects flow and how distinctly the possibility of
thought follows. The viewer on her model is in no doubt that they felt
something; they know for sure that they have been affected by what
they see. Foster, as I understand it, is trying to query this certainty.
Thus the image does not seize hold of the viewer in a violent or possessive way (it does not shock or otherwise overwhelm us with
emotion), but occupies a place somewhere beyond perception (the
image has been formally registered by our senses) and consciousness
(but it fails to register enough for thought or indeed feeling to hold it
fast). It is an experience with radically uncertain feeling, not the clear
economy of affect governing Bennett's model; it really is not real in
the sense imagined by Bennett.

So while the viewer is touched by the image they, nevertheless, remain unsure whether they have or have not been touched by it: at issue, then, is a responsibility for images that do not mean that much to the viewer, which is to say images that elicit our response without our knowing for certain why. The image stops or pulls short of affect and cognition; hence the sense of the image is not or cannot be fully redeemed by thought or feeling. It is not given thought or feeling. In sum, there is no satisfactory sense of the image or sense of personal attachment, which as I have argued above is not the case for Bennett, for whom the viewer is very personally – and I hazard satisfactorily – caught up in the drama of affect, even if held at a certain distance by the formalism of the image. But this 'lack' of personal commitment or satisfactory return is, in fact, politically vital, precisely because it agitates thought without the subject really knowing that they are bothered at all. For Bennett the viewer knows quite clearly that they are troubled by the image, since they can trace the source of their agitation to the formalism of the image, which in the case of Favero was the use of juxtaposition of love and hate which is understood by Bennett to get the viewer immediately thinking about the moral landscape of incest. But Foster is suggesting a process less certain and evident than this when he is discussing traumatic realism in reference to pop art and repetition, for as I understand it *The Evil One* can be read as making us ask, 'have I thought (about this image) at all?'

CHAPTER 4

All Trauma, Talk and Tears: In the Event of Speaking Out on TV

Not so long ago it was *not* 'too far-fetched to imagine daytime talk as the electronic syndicated version of consciousness-raising groups of the women's movements' (Mellencamp 1988, cited in Shattuc 1997). Today, it would stretch the imagination. Instead, the success of daytime talk and the daily parade of women offering testimony to painful realities serve for many critics as perhaps the best example for demonstrating the limits if not outright failure of a cultural politics of trauma. Take, for example, Frigga Haug's socialist feminist reading of the contemporary scene of speaking out, and her attempt 'to demonstrate a relationship between sex scandals and the demands and opportunities of the global free markets' (2001: 55). Importantly, Haug begins with an anecdote concerning a trip she made to Toronto almost ten years previously. She recalls how having landed in Canada she found herself 'greeted by lots of TV programmes blaring all over the place', which she would have ignored if she had not had to wait for her luggage. So, with a view to 'inhal[ing]' her 'first English/ Canadian in preparation for the months to come', she took a closer look: 'There were two women on the screen, one of them crying, the other encouraging her with a voice habituated to offering commodities to go on to dig deeper, to reveal and confess' (ibid.). Initially, Haug recounts a struggle to 'understand the crying woman' which was only resolved when 'the showmistress interrupted the whole scene, took a book from a nearby table and encouraged all of us to come out to reveal our secret that we had all been abused as children', and 'if we were not sure we could read all about it in the book' she was offering on sale for 100 Canadian dollars. At this point Haug left the airport and promptly 'forgot the scene on the TV' (ibid.).

Despite immediately forgetting this scene – which clearly represents the confessional culture and the commodified conditions of women's testimony to sexual abuse – it returned to haunt Haug during her stay as a visiting professor at the Ontario Institute for Studies in Education, for when she took her place among the feminist faculty and student body, she found herself party to a seemingly endless series of incest disclosures. In response, she was initially speechless, but with every passing disclosure she gradually began to experience a growing scepticism in the face of the demand that she believe 'that almost every girl in Canada was in some way or other a victim of sexual abuse by her uncle or father' (ibid.). This creeping doubt with regard to the 'success' of a feminist politics of speaking out was compounded by her contrasting experiences of teaching an 'advanced sociological theory' course, 'which went very well: the students argued different positions on a very abstract level and seemed to learn a lot', and teaching a memory course, which was a 'catastrophe'. 'I wanted to discuss memory work', Haug recalls, but instead with 'more than 50 students [. . .] squeezed into a room too small for this number [. . .] they yelled at me. They refused to do memory work'. Or rather they refused to do it until they had 'demanded special measures of safety. Asked for at least two additional therapists and wanted to know if I could handle [it]'. It took, she recalls, 'three weeks to understand that they had self-evidently assumed memory work meant that they would be expected to reveal an incestuous past, an idea that they found fascinating and horrible in equal measure' (ibid.).

By this stage in her visit, Haug was experiencing ever-deepening suspicions about – and resistance to – the daily tide of testimony she was hearing, so in an attempt to test her perception of the apparently scandalous scale of sexual abuse in Canada, she 'brought the subject up in the "Feminist Focus" group and found out that, of course, everybody was an incest survivor except one' (ibid.: 57). At no point did she experience any querying of the reality of the prevalence of sexual abuse, until

> some time later I met a student who wanted to write her thesis on feminist therapy and sexual abuse. She confessed that she had wanted to criticise the total obsession of all feminist therapy and politics with abuse, but she did not dare to do so. (ibid.)

Finally, Haug heard a dissenting opinion, which not only reflected her own doubts over the relationship between feminism, psychotherapy and sexual abuse (which include, for her, the seemingly contradictory appeal of discovering a history of incest) but allowed her to explicitly narrate her anxiety concerning the paradoxical alignment of feminism with the moral majority (in that both support state intervention), whereupon Haug concluded her anecdote by admitting that 'the contradictions also caused a rupture within myself. Such a strange situation urgently needed an analytical approach' (ibid.).

Ten years later Haug's 'Sexual Deregulation, or, The Child Abuser as Hero in Neoliberalism' stands as her analytical response to the 'strange situation'. In light of her anecdote, it is not surprising that her article constitutes a provocative engagement with the issues thrown up by her visit to Canada. So while Haug is careful to note in her abstract that 'This subject is so emotionally charged that a rational discussion of that which goes beyond our comprehension is almost impossible' and the 'sets of complex interrelated issues associated with child sexual abuse deny any simple description or critique', she is, nonetheless, keen to 'enable a new perspective and facilitate thinking' (ibid.: 55) by approaching the topic via Ian Hacking's work on memory politics, Foucault's work on sexuality and the operations of modern power, and finally the media case against Marc Dutroux, the Belgian paedophile. Although claiming the work of Hacking and Foucault as the conceptual bases for her analysis of the Dutroux case, her approach and her use of their work is underpinned by the historical materialism key to her original work on memory, an influence entirely missed by the Canadian students. Consequently she figures the problems raised by the Canadian trip as a question not simply about confessional culture but also as a question over the 'relationship between changes in sexual politics and how we think about drives in the context of their relation to neoliberalism', where 'drives' will be read by her as economic or material in nature as well as sexual. In sum, then, the article provides a political economy critique of speaking out and sexual abuse.

There is no doubt that Haug's attempt to provide a materialist critique of speaking out stands as a powerfully cogent critique of the liberal individualism underwriting the feminist politics of speaking about sexual abuse (which includes, for example, the idea that speaking is an expression of the privilege of being free or that as individuals we have a unique store of experiences and memories). Yet I also want to query the terms of Haug's analysis, for while it is in many places acutely insightful why is it so easy to forget the woman crying on the TV? Is there nothing (more) to say about her? Is it not possible that she could trouble the terms of Haug's analysis if given a chance to speak? In an attempt to answer these questions, this chapter will supplement Haug's anecdotal dismissal with an analysis of women's talk-show testimony to sexual abuse. Key to this talk-show analysis is the question of how we might understand the political significance of women's on-air testimony. In a manner of speaking, this might, of course, be a way of asking the impossible: why do women cry on TV, and who are they when they speak; or conversely, why do women speak, and who are they when they cry?

Five years after the English translation of her 1980s groundbreaking commentary on memory work – *Female Sexualization: A Collective Work of Memory* (Haug et al. 1987) – Haug found herself in 1990s Canada puzzled by the fact that memory work translated so readily as a quest into exploring one's personal history, a history already anticipated as harrowing and leading straight to incest. Troubling Haug was the fact that students could think about working through the past only according to the seemingly ideologically individualistic and universalising precepts of psychotherapy (hence according to Haug the students did not appear concerned about the world beyond them, while at the same time appearing to expect that all memory work leads to sexual abuse having taken place), when originally memory work was designed as *a collective, socialist feminist* process for exploring 'women's capacity – or incapacity – for action and for happiness' (1987: 33). Indeed, for Haug, the idea that exploring the personal past could be a *collaborative* and politically *socialist* informed quest for happiness appeared lost on the students in the classroom. Yet back in the early 1980s the very possibility of countering 'unhappiness with the struggle for the capacity to be happy' (ibid.: 34) was a collective struggle for Haug and her fellow feminist collaborators. 'It was as a collective that we recorded and analysed our personal memories' (ibid.: 36), since remembering collectively was the only way of assessing the *indelibly social* nature of memory. As Haug argues, 'The mass character of social processes is obliterated within the concept of individuality' (ibid.: 43), and more pointedly, for

Haug, 'the notion of the uniqueness of experience and of the various ways in which it is consciously accessed is a fiction' (ibid.). On both counts, then, working through the traumatic memories of incest might be understood to figure as a fiction in the sense that psychotherapy carries with it the notion that our memories are uniquely are own, especially when they are traumatic, and, then, additionally, the notion that psychotherapy can access and deliver this past to us as individuals is a subsequent delusion. Here, then, the fiction that Haug objects to, and the fiction she presumes to be held by the students, is the idea that we each have in our possession a private and deeply held set of personal experiences and memories which uniquely make us who we are; we would not be without them.

In light of this understanding, it is no surprise that Haug struggles with the fact that the students appeared to prefer a method of working through their own trauma with the aid of psychotherapists than doing general memory work with a pedagogue, especially given the fact that memory work was conceived by Haug and the collective she worked with as a guard against the seductions of 'vulgar psychoanalytic models of interpretation' (ibid.: 56) and 'amateur psychotherapy' (ibid.: 57). For Haug, the only point of memory was to analyse and learn as a collective (subject): impersonally. Importantly, then, for Haug, memory work was based on adopting the 'standpoint of others' (ibid.: 58). It is this ability to think abstractly about one's personal memories that Haug perceived to be missing among the students taking her memory class in Canada in the 1990s. This loss of critical distance and with it the capacity for thinking is symbolically represented by the fact that while the social theory students were capable of taking up 'different positions on a very abstract level', hence learning 'a lot', the memory students were not. They figure instead as being incapable of taking up any position other than their own, and certainly, then, not capable of taking it up on an abstract level. Thinking about one's own past appears, here, to be thinking precious little. There appears nothing much to be learnt about ourselves and our place in the world if we are drawn into that world according to the precepts of psychotherapy, which is why Haug maintains that we should not 'allow ourselves to be ruled by what the therapeutic institutions suggest to us about ourselves' (Haug 2001: 60). Thus she draws on the Canadian philosopher Ian

Hacking (1995) to argue that 'to reconstruct oneself in a history of abuse results in an action-impaired and difficult personality of the kind that is the starting point rather than the goal of memory work' (Haug 2001: 59).

For Hacking and Haug both, psychotherapeutic discourse prospers on privileging the idea of an all too deeply and personally held past from which a sense of distance appears necessarily impossible, and thus does not provide occasion for what in the early 1980s Haug had termed 'living historically'. The idea of 'living historically' is key to Haug, since it means among other things 'to signal our desire to change our constricting conditions to make the world a more habitable place' (Haug et al. 1987: 50–1). In short, living historically is to live as a globally responsible citizen; working through does not provide the necessary conditions for doing so. Working through, it might be said here, works to produce self-absorbed, unthinking and morally bankrupt individuals. Bearing in mind the politically transparent terms of Haug's original 1980s project on memory work and the classroom scenario of seemingly adolescent and unreasonable students, it is hard not to be persuaded by Haug's critique, although I will aim to disrupt its cogency.

Although sharing a set of concerns with Hacking, Haug is a little more precisely concerned to explore why we are losing the desire for 'living historically' at this very particular point in time, and how this loss might relate to the changing nature of state power and economic relations in late modernity. In order to explore this problem, Haug shifts the terms of her analysis to the work of Foucault, for although Hacking's analysis is fundamentally informed by Foucault's insights, it cannot substitute, Haug maintains, for Foucault's thinking around 'sexual abuse, which might drive one's disquieting thoughts about the sudden emergence of the issue of abuse and its association with inquiries about the soul into a different direction' (2001: 60). For Haug, what is most immediately important about Foucault's work is that he relocates 'sexual abuse within the family' and thus 'refocuses our view from the deviant individual abuse and his drives to a particular institution, the family' (ibid.), whereupon the family functions as a key site for the working of modern power. The family, especially in issues of sexuality, is a privileged nexus for a microphysics of power. In other words, by placing sex in the family, power devolves responsibility to the parents, who become liable for policing the sexuality of children at home. Thus power extends its grip and it does so economically. Although, given this is Foucault speaking here, the policing of innocence incites its trespass: repression acts as the agency for expression.

In addition to Foucault's insights into the workings of modern power and the place of sex, Haug acknowledges the importance of his commentary on the counterproductive nature of speaking out about the sexually intimate violence of incest and rape. Sexual violence narratives do not stand outside power, but rather they are 'permeated by the very microphysics of power' (ibid.: 64). Therefore, Haug argues, they are used

> in well-rehearsed ways: the whipping up of sexual desire by a detailed description of what happened, the production of a single culprit and, above all, the discovery of sex as the beginning and the reason for all pathologies in the individual and in society. The efforts of liberation are incorporated into the original deployment. (ibid.)

In keeping, then, with many other feminists, Haug is acknowledging how women's testimony to sexual abuse can be recuperated by modern power, but she also expresses a concern over what she takes to be the apparent futility of resistance. Thus she writes:

> Although Foucault shows very exciting shifts by introducing a positivity of power, the network of supporting and resisting points is so tight that there is no escape. It is a network of domination that is woven and maintained in participation with the oppressed themselves; in such constructions every exit seems to be blocked, there is no space for any intervening thinking and action that is not at the same time the back side of the very power against which it proceeds and therefore a supporting part of it. (ibid.: 65)

Keen to develop the possibility for resignifying power beyond the model of individual responses that she finds in Foucault's work, Haug argues that:

> Countermodels as such can come only out of a movement – from initiatives, from groups, not individuals . . . to transgress silence in a

direction in which speaking out is a communication with others on the road to more self-determined forms of individuality and forms to live another kind of society from below. (ibid.: 66)

Indeed, Haug considers it a vital time for collective action, since modern power is in crisis. Crucially, she writes that it is now 'possible that the very relations of power that determine sex deployment are no longer tolerable in their current form' (ibid.: 64). Indeed, as

much as campaigns about the deployment of sexuality (like violence against women, abuse, sexual harassment) conceal or hide the ruptures, rejections, breaks, crises and breakdowns of the old order at large, they are at the same time an indicator that a certain type of power, a dominant deployment of ruling and order, is breaking down. (ibid.: 67)

Thus she argues the 'important question is how much this crisis of the former "new procedures of power" can be used to come close to [the panoply] of human rights' (ibid.). In respect of this seeming reconfiguration of the relations of modern power, Haug is not looking, then, to simply replicate the insights and methodological strategy governing her original project on memory, nor simply looking to reproduce the insights of Hacking or Foucault, but situate the explosion of sexual abuse memory in relation to the globally changing nature of state power and capitalist relations. Thus she is also asking why 'These sexual and political scandals and the politics they have inflamed coincide with a time when neoliberalism is generating global change on a scale not dissimilar to the industrial revolution' (ibid.: 68).

In an attempt to answer these questions, Haug's analysis proceeds by juxtaposing media response to the Marc Dutroux case, the Belgian paedophile whose story 'reveals itself as a product of the disintegration of the Belgian state' (ibid.: 69), and the media reporting of a UNICEF conference on the sexual exploitation of children. The Dutroux case, Haug argues, was reported, at least initially, in the language of the pathological sex offender, while the UNICEF conference was reported in terms of 'exploitation and profit, trade and material gain' (ibid.: 70). Increasingly, however, she argues the reporting of the Dutroux became confusing as reporters struggled to account for the role of accomplices and gangs – for the networked, profit-oriented nature of the case, considerations that defied 'the reports and discussions that usually govern debates about sexual abuse' (ibid.: 70). On the other hand, 'The language used at the conference is unambiguous and clear. [. . .] What becomes abundantly clear is that this is not about perverts but about markets and profits; about exploitation and children as objects of trade' (ibid.: 71). 'From this position of profit on the world market', Haug argues, 'the mysterious Dutroux case is easily decipherable: we're dealing with an internationally operating, lucrative business which combines with other forms of criminality' (ibid.), and it 'is obvious that the question whether or not Dutroux is a paedophile and has socially unacceptable interests in children is of negligible interest within this morass of exploitation and profit' (ibid.: 72).

Following these observations, Haug argues that 'we are unexpectedly directed towards a political economy of power. Such deeds – that is, such synergy or collaboration [between individual and state perversion] – are likely to occur everywhere where there is a power-political vacuum because of state debt' (ibid.: 74). Today, then, we are dealing with a distinctly 'profit-oriented version of child abuse' which extends way beyond the political question of the family (ibid.). Thus Haug argues the

> objectification that precedes the marketing of female bodies and those children reveals the structural problem. Women and children are considered property, wares, things, without rights: mere bodies that have to be pressed into service for maximum profit. This structure allows the return to our usual ways of thinking about the abuse of children in families and away from the international trade in children. (ibid.)

As a consequence, Haug argues, 'The outrage against individualised misdeeds masks large-scale crime as it currently occurs under the heading neoliberalism or liberalisation of the markets' (ibid.: 68). Ultimately linking the scene from the airport to how the mass media report organised sex crimes in terms of the individual (thus failing to grasp the globally systemic nature of child sexual abuse), Haug concludes that 'the seeming normalcy of power over other people, the degradation of people to mere objects of lust, is no longer viewed as a structural problem of capitalist societies', and therefore it 'is still the case that we need to overthrow all those conditions that make human beings lead a degraded, enslaved and humiliating existence' (ibid.: 76).

In no uncertain terms, Haug is keen to highlight the structural and distinctly global market nature of child abuse and in so doing to demonstrate how our preoccupation with the individual (whether victim or perpetrator) occludes our view of globally systemic capital-based injustice. It is, she argues, simply a matter of bringing this reality into view to gain an understanding of the bigger picture. 'We don't need to take a theoretically sophisticated road to get there', she writes, because 'Material reality forces us to see these matters as they are. In the third world families sell women and children because it is their only means of survival. They effectively act as slave traders. Young women fetch between $1000 and $2000' (ibid.: 74). By concluding her analysis with these stark economic indicators it is difficult to resist the ultimate logic of Haug's argument, which by necessity would have us reassess the significance of the fact that women in the first world are being exhorted to remember their pain for 100 Canadian dollars. What, Haug seems to be asking, is the real cost of remembering sexual abuse in the first world? What, indeed, is the price of remembering, speaking and crying in the relative freedom of an advanced capitalist society? These are deadly serious questions that require asking, and Haug's response serves as a compelling answer: the price is the reproduction of a profoundly immoral system of economic and social hardship. Put brutally, if following Haug's argument, some young women will not have the luxury of sitting in a classroom to remember their trauma let alone make demands for special safety measures, and some women will not have the opportunity to appear on TV to cry 'freely' over their experiences. On both counts, it is the privilege of one or two lone individuals. To her credit, then, Haug sets this truth before us.

But what, then, are we supposed to do with those lone individuals speaking out about their pain in the glare of the mass media? How, for example, are we to read the testimony of Sabine Dardenne, who, on 28 May 1996, was kidnapped by Dutroux and thereby, as she puts it, lived this piece of Belgium history 'from the inside' (2004: 4)? How are we meant to explain her desire to 'retrace her stations of the cross' in order that the Belgian state government does not forget its duty to protect society against individuals like Dutroux? Might it not be useful, at this point, to remind Haug of her own conclusion in 1987: that

> there might well be no single, 'true' method that is alone appropriate to this kind of work. What we need is imagination. We can, perhaps, say quite decisively that the very heterogeneity of everyday life demands similarly heterogeneous methods if it is to be understood. (1987: 71)

I am looking to push Haug's original insight back into the arena of contemporary analysis because I remain convinced that despite the cogency of her analysis of the global nature of child abuse, it lacks the imaginative impulse of her earlier work, and thus it costs us the possibility of knowing some other equally valid truth, even when that truth might be the unknowing of truth. For what do we really gain if the misery of some is gauged by comparing its value in exchange for the misery of others (100 versus 1000–2000)? When a woman crying on TV is shown as an example to the silent suffering of mass, anonymous others? Indeed, is there not a sense in which the terms of Haug's calculus reflect the very economy of profit and loss that she is seeking to critique, such that, for example, the 'freedom' of Canadian women to speak about incest – whether on television or in the classroom – is gained at the enslavement of third world women; the success of a feminist campaign against patriarchal abuses has been at the cost of a Marxist analysis of economic oppression; a pedagogical emphasis on the domestic and personal has been traded for an emphasis on the global and structurally abstract? Is this not a particularly punitive form of analysis?

These questions are not raised to simply dismiss the concerns of Haug or imply that women's testimony to sexual abuse cannot be subject to critical thinking. Indeed, we should ask why Dardenne's book – *I Choose to Live* – has become a best-seller, having been published and reprinted six times in one year. There is an appetite for this book which is problematic. Women's memory and testimony are not sacrosanct. But by the same token, the historical and economic conditions understood to be determining the production of women's memory and testimony are themselves not sacrosanct: the analytical primacy of capitalism, neoliberalism and global free markets can be queried without the charge of political naivety being levelled. Indeed, here the issue of what is sacrosanct, ethical and historically determining is distinctly important, since, as Avita Ronell argues, television is symbolically linked to 'the image-laden New Testament'. Television is an image-based, anti-sacral technology, and thus 'our being has been modalized by a technology that works according to a different protocol of ethical attunement' which is necessary to remember if we are to understand 'the site of testimony that television has initiated' (1994: 281). In the age of 'blaring TVs' the significance of women giving testimony, especially when sobbing in the process, requires careful, yet critically imaginative, ways of reckoning, since television has fundamentally altered what it means to bear witness to suffering in late modernity. It is not enough to simply dismiss the image based on a language originally developed to think through the implications of the last industrial revolution.

At issue, then, is how 'to calculate' (the cost of) pain in an age of 'blaring TVs' without a fixing of (the material) meaning of suffering or, as Ronell asserts, while recognising reality 'is no longer appropriable as a phenomenon of essence' (ibid.: 284). If the politics of giving sexual abuse testimony is more complex than Haug seems to allow, feminism might yet be advised to take a new, if not necessarily sophisticated, theoretical road 'to get there', since not only does the notion of what constitutes 'there' change when the reality question is traumatic, but our ability to perceive what is 'there' has also changed in the age of 'blaring TVs', for we live, as Ronell asserts, '[i]n an era of constitutive opaqueness' (ibid.: 281). Hence, 'we dwell not in transcendental light but in the shadows of mediation and withdrawal [and thus] there will be no revelation, can be no manifestation as such – things have to be tuned in, adjusted, subjected to double-takes' (ibid.: 291). Pace Haug, the reality of oppression is not bathed in a 'natural' (third world?) light for all to see but exists, inevitably now for most feminist critics, in the (first world?) glow emanating from the TV screen, and as such the reality of systemic suffering does not simply reveal itself to us. Reality, no matter how stark the economic indicators may be, has to be made out and not assumed. To my mind, however, Haug fails to grasp the importance of this historical change and how feminist understanding of women's testimony in the age of 'blaring TVs' will require an alternative language, if a possibly blasphemous language. There is no simple recourse to the language of Marxism or historical materialism. Indeed, as Donna Haraway argues, blasphemy might be key if we are to build 'political myth[s] faithful to feminism, socialism and materialism'. She writes:

> Blasphemy has always seemed to require taking things very seriously. I know no better stance to adopt from within the secular-religious, evangelical traditions of United State politics, including the politics of socialist feminism. [. . .] Blasphemy is not apostasy. Irony is about contradictions that do not resolve into larger wholes, even dialectically, about the tension of holding incompatible things together because both or all are necessary and true. (Irony is about humour and serious play. It is a rhetorical strategy and a political method [. . .].) (1991: 149)

It is no doubt 'necessary and true' to establish the significance of women's talk-show testimony according to the language of socialist feminism (and hence in the context of neoliberalism and global capitalism). Yet it is also equally 'necessary and true' to establish the significance of Dardenne's memoir and women's TV testimony according to the language of past trauma – although doing so while disrupting the recuperative logic of modern power, which if Haug is right is the moment to be contemplating a renewed project. Famously, of course, Haraway places the image of the cyborg at the centre of her 'ironic faith', whereas I want to place the image of the women speaking and crying on talk shows at the centre of mine. To this end, then, I want to 'tune' back into the phenomenon of women's daytime talk, 'adjust' the terms of political thinking and subject the spectacle of women's TV testimony to a distinctly irreverent, profane double take.

In March 2002 the BBC late morning talk show *Kilroy* aired with a show dedicated to sexual abuse. 'Sexual Abuse in the Family' is typical of its genre (although possibly nowhere near the worst of its kind), with the host – Kilroy-Silk – announcing the theme of the show with the rhetorical – 'Tell me something, do *you* think *you'd* know if *your* man was sexually abusing *your* children?' – a provocation that is immediately followed up as he moves centre-stage with the slightly more respectfully intoned and more widely addressed:

> Do *you* realize that 70% of all sexual abuse cases occur within the family, so would *you* know whether *your* man was abusing *your* children? How do *you* cope when *you* are the victim of sexual abuse by a member of *your* family? How do *you* make people listen when *your* father or step-father is sexually abusing *you*?

Any pretence, however, that this introduction might be laying the groundwork for a faintly feminist discussion of sexual abuse with its acknowledgement that most child abuse takes place in the home and is committed by fathers is quickly laid to rest when Kilroy-Silk moves with barely a break in his delivery to ask the first speaker about her experiences of abuse: 'Nicola, your father abused you, what happened?' In response to this question the young woman provides a vague and somewhat shaky answer about her father abusing her that quickly solicits another question from Kilroy-Silk: 'How old?' Although sounding an innocuous enough probe it, nonetheless, evidences his desire for knowing ever more precise and further detail, an interrogative dynamic that informs the production of her testimony: 'But what age were you [. . . when he actually started]?' 'What was he doing [when you say doing "not very nice things"]?' 'He was touching you [. . . where]?' 'Did it go any way further [. . . than just his touching you]?' Eventually, Nicola concedes to Kilroy-Silk's hidden yet structuring question: 'No, he didn't rape me, but perhaps could have if given the opportunity.'

Thus Kilroy-Silk moves quickly among the predominantly female audience in what is for the most part a clearly orchestrated set of movements and with what are for the most part an equally rehearsed set of questions which either silently carry the desire to know 'but did he actually rape you as a child' or less silently carry the desire to provoke controversy as he actively encourages the women to openly contradict each other and the 'experts', in this instance, charity workers, solicitors and a token MP. Indeed, as the only named participants, the experts appear on the show to provide professional and apparently reasonable – if at times less than welcome – opinion, including, for example, the importance of maintaining a tariff system as legal doctrine (shorter sentences for pleading guilty, longer sentences for more 'serious' abuse). The commentary serves as the perfect foil for the 'ill-informed', 'irrational' objections of the women who make 'soap box' speeches about how men's prison sentences are nothing in comparison to their sentences of lifetime suffering. Indeed, at one point, the conflict of opinion generated by the show risks descending into utter chaos as one of the women – identified as an incest survivor and rape counsellor – repeatedly and vehemently refuses the right of the MP to talk about offender rehabilitation schemes, until Kilroy-Silk asserts his authority to allow the man to speak. Indeed, the idea of rehabilitation is a point of repeated discussion with one woman, predictably perhaps, preferring more draconian measures: castration is mooted as a possibility.

In addition to this media cocktail of charged and seemingly unreasonable sentiment, there is also intrigue. Thus we listen to the testimony given anonymously by a mother admitting to the fact that she failed to protect her daughter, who by all accounts is so badly traumatised that a therapist refused the mother's money for the counselling of the child. Then there is the mystery generated as one of the women describes how she was rigged with a hidden camera so she could secretly film her father abusing her – which Kilroy-Silk admits to seeing when he lets it be known that the filming had been done for another TV programme in order to both expose the father and provide material evidence for the police, who had been particularly remiss in this case. And while not a commercial channel broadcast, there are nonetheless 'breaks' in the talking as Kilroy-Silk addresses the camera to 'advertise' a crisis helpline for sexual abuse victims and a future show on 'false accusation' that Kilroy-Silk insists is not meant to be provocative and in no way is meant to cast judgement on anything being said by the women in the studio. The show eventually closes with Kilroy-Silk emphasising that *you* do not need to suffer in silence, and with a parting flourish insisting once more that the helpline number is put back up on the screen, whereupon he ends the show with his trademark: 'take care of *yourself*'.

Given this account of *Kilroy*'s 'Sexual Abuse in the Family', it is evident why talk shows have been so easy to critique: the women are goaded into making a spectacle of themselves, especially when arguing with each other over their experiences, which by turn works to reveal the limits of a politics based on deeply personal memory. There is little to no rational or systematic analysis of male power; indeed, quite the contrary, with Kilroy-Silk clearly enjoying the privileges of male power when looking to elicit salacious detail and when choosing to silence the women. There is no attempt to extrapolate from the particular and hence no attempt to establish a sense of common reality. There is no discussion of radical solutions or collective strategies for change. Despite taking up the floor as a group of women, they each appear only to speak in person, and thus this hardly figures as a version of a consciousness-raising group – even allowing for the fact that in practice the groups did not live up to their own ideals. *Kilroy*'s 'Sexual Abuse in Family' is a mockery of this ideal, replacing it instead with the 'animated, messy' talk of television (Squire 1997: 99).

This point is made by Louise Armstrong, who was, in fact, the first incest survivor to speak on a talk show when she appeared on the US broadcast *The Today Show* in 1978, in the hope of effecting change. Signalling her collapsing faith in the possibility of women's testimony, Armstrong maintains that 'talk shows, which, in their early days, had appeared to be a medium through which issues could be aired, [have become], in effect, a medium through which issues are encapsulated and neutralised' (1994: 175). Thus Armstrong argues there is no content to women's on-air testimony, or if there is any content its significance is altered by a lack of 'context' (ibid.). There is 'nothing to lend the issue[s] "coherence" or "connection" with any other issue[s], nothing to signal significance or intent' (ibid.). Thus women's talk-show testimony to sexual abuse is simply 'played out as personal stories in a framework that [is] constructed to emphasize emotionality over rationality; to contain personal stories, not to extend them to include larger meaning' (ibid.: 174). Indeed, with the power to prevent the conversion of women's personal testimony into a social and political discourse on male violence, talk shows are free to 'air trivia alongside discontent alongside tragedy: inflating the small and diminishing the great into one huge watery soup – offering passive observance of virtual reality' (ibid.: 175). Here, then, according to Armstrong, women's talk-show testimony is *insignificant* because it is held captive by the sensationalism of media interest with victim and wider public interest 'thriving' on an empty, trivial(ising) diet of personal stories. In short, women's talk-show testimony has no *substance*, becoming instead *mere words* such that any possibility of inaugurating rational discussion will always dissolve into a 'hulla-baloo' (ibid.: 7). With an inevitable despair, Armstrong is left to argue that speaking out has become a commodity with the 'bankable' nature of women's pain signalling the 'bankrupt' nature of a radical feminist politics of testifying to traumatic experiences (ibid.: 205). Useless, in other words.

In a sense, Armstrong's concerns about the power of women's testimony to reference the reality of sexual abuse are reflected on *Kilroy* by the woman responsible for haranguing the MP. Joining in on a rolling conversation about the problems of forging adult, inti-mate relationships, the woman begins by describing how she has two children, but has struggled to maintain any long-term rela-tionships. This said, however, she admits to having recently estab-lished a new relationship which is, she says, a 'whole new ball game', requiring that she 'learn new feelings' and 'new curves'. 'Silly, really', she says. At this point her flowing narrative is sud-denly broken, as she quickly – and as if in explanation as to 'why silly' – insists:

> I was three when my father raped me . . . He'd take me to fields, he raped me in fields and I say rape because I mean rape. It is not just something that's . . . um, we're . . . we use that word abuse, it's not abuse, it is rape, it's disgraceful, it's disgusting. You look at every-body. [. . .] I remember this old man walking past when my father was having sex with me in this field, I remember feeling so ashamed, I was 'Oh my God, this guy, this man, is thinking the old man is having sex with me' . . .

At this point, predictably, Kilroy-Silk interjects:

> 'What age were . . . what age?'
> 'I was twelve, about twelve.'

Initially, as I have just suggested, the woman's testimony to her experience of being raped as a three-year-old child serves as an explanation for why the difficulty of forging an intimate relationship might seem silly. Yet her testimony quickly turns into a discourse on the accuracy and adequacy of language to demonstrate the reality of which she and the others speak. 'Abuse' does not cover it. Rape does, since it does justice to the fact that it is a disgraceful, disgusting violation, which by turn gives force to the impact it has had on her subsequent life. Politically, the word 'rape' is key since it serves to rewrite the original scene, which originally she could only understand through the eyes of another as a sex scene, yet knew for herself not to be, but could not express.

But despite what is an apparent confidence in the power of words to name reality, the very fact of her having to vouch for the meaning of the word 'rape' suggests otherwise. Years later she is still looking to secure the 'sex' scene as a scene of violence by having us see it through the language of rape. Language and meaning, as she knows only too well, and is looking to exploit to a certain extent, is slippery. This inability to secure the terms of her testimony and thereby our perception of reality is brought home by the apparent inconsistency of her account of when she was raped, which slips from the emphatic three to the indecisive 'twelve, about twelve'. Once again, when she is put on the spot, she finds it difficult to secure an accurate perspective. Was she or was she not raped at three? Or was it that she was 'abused' at the age of three but it felt like rape? Is she employing rape as a metaphor for the horror she felt as a child when her father used to take her out into the fields to abuse her? Rape her? Is she retroactively supplanting the 'reality' of later experiences onto earlier, yet different ones? Whatever the answer to these questions – and whether or not they are useful questions to begin with – it remains evident that it is difficult to maintain an 'insider's' perspective, to secure, in any way, the view of the reality from the 'inside'. She is being forced to take a distance from herself and thereby take up the outsider's perspective, which appears in the studio and in the fields to belie a prurient interest. The word 'rape' does not have the power to give us the inside track on the trauma of violence.

This inability to secure the terms of her experience is given symbolic and literal weight by the fact that the above testimony, although sounding as if she is continuously talking live on air, is, in fact, an edited version. On closer and repeated listening it is evident that in production her testimony has been cut and spliced at vital points. Her narrative about being raped at three and the inadequacy of language does not appear intended by her as an answer to the 'silly, really' question of forging adult intimate relations, although clearly it serves as a nicely dramatic answer for the *Kilroy* production staff. One can only guess that she was rather more prosaic in explaining why it is difficult to play the game of adult love. But stripped of its original context, her reasoning can never be known. The original footage is lost to us and presumably all concerned in reality and in memory. Would even she remember?

At this juncture, however, I want to stake my argument carefully. My point is not to insist that her 'authentic' and original testimony has been altered and corrupted by media production and that we only need to restore its 'proper context' to establish its meaning, but rather that we would be compelled to guess the meaning anyway. Language cannot secure the inside track on reality. The woman could, indeed, talk, and talk she did, but this does not bring her or us any closer to the meaning of her experience. Which is not to say that there cannot be meaning, but it is unintended at best. So, for example, when Kilroy-Silk asks her how old she was, his questioning is surely redundant, given how clearly she had stated that she was three. Notwithstanding the possibility that he is simply being gratuitous in asking, the apparent incongruity is due again to editing. Thus we do not know which question is answered by 'Twelve, about twelve'. Maybe: 'What age were you when you told someone?' '. . . When you sought help?', '. . . When you fought back?' '. . . When you knew it to be rape?' In the absence of the original footage, we do not know whether these might have been the original questions. In other words, we do not know the significance of the gap between the years three and twelve. But what we do know, and we know this despite the censoring of her testimony, is that she could talk and talk, only stopping when she feels the need to shout over people. 'You are a nightmare is what you are,' Kilroy-Silk complains when he fails, yet again, to stop her having her say.

Ultimately, this is not confessional talk in structure. This is speaking in excess of itself, pure utterance – which is not to say that only the fact of talking matters, for, as Judith Butler argues:

there are differences of opinions about how to deal with 'content' or with the surface meaning of the utterance. But one thing seems clear, which is the content, the intended meaning, cannot be fully over-come or transcended, since how one utters that content, or what the uttering of that content does, will probably comment on the content, will probably comment on the intention that bears the content along. (ibid.: 171–2)

How does the woman's incessant talking comment on the inade-quacy of language to secure the reality of violence? She is saying two things: first, she is expressing a frustration about the conveyance of meaning and its ability to change situations, as Armstrong so clearly expresses. But second, and all the while, she is still banking on lan-guage, still willing to bet that things can change. It might not make sense in the terms established by Armstrong and it certainly lacks political meaning or substance in the way she formally understood it. But language has a power not reducible to patent meaning, a power not easily measured in instrumental terms, as a known and measurable quantity. It's called shouting the odds. Silly, really.

This is all well and good, but the idea that speaking out might promote prurient and voyeuristic desire remains a concern, and it is key to the argument made by Linda Alcoff and Linda Gray in their influential 'Survivor Discourse: Transgression or Recuperation'. Like Armstrong, Alcoff and Gray are at pains to argue that women's testimony 'has been sensationalized and exploited by the mass media, in fictional dramatizations as well as "journalistic" formats such as the Geraldo Rivera and Phil Donahue television talk shows' (1993: 262). Illustrating their critique of the commercial interest in speaking out about sexual abuse, Alcoff and Gray discuss an ABC talk show dedicated to the subject of university campus rape which included two student activists from their own university, one of whom had been a rape victim. Typically, Alcoff and Gray argue, the show focused on the victim – Tracey – by zooming in on her in close-up yet refusing her the opportunity to dictate the terms of her own testimony, seeking instead details about the rape. 'What did this show do?' ask Alcoff and Gray. It made the victim 'an object of analy-sis [and because the] camera insistently cut away to Tracey's face even when others were speaking' it also made a general ' "example" ' of her (ibid.: 276). As they argue, talk shows 'display the emotions of survivors for public consumption' by following a typical format where

> at the start of the show survivors are shown in close-up, 'telling their stories' [whereupon] the host of the show makes sure to ask questions that are sufficiently probing to get the survivors to cry on screen ([a process that can be] accomplished by discovering their most vulnerable issues in a preshow interview and then keying in when cameras are rolling). (ibid.: 277)

Thus the victim is put on complete show. In 'a culture where audience sensations are dulled by graphic depictions of violence (both real and fictional on television) and in which mass sensibilities have atrophied under conditions of late capitalism', Alcoff and Gray argue 'these shows provide a moment in which real, raw, and intense feelings can be observed and in some cases remembered. This emotional "shock value" is their use value as a media commodity' (ibid.: 278).

Unlike Armstrong, however, who figures media and public interest as somewhat indifferent and passive consumption (we listen, but pay no particular interest; it is a distracted interest), Alcoff and Gray figure viewer interest in distinctly more worrying terms when they argue that the presence of survivors and a focus on 'the details of the violations with close-ups of survivors' anguished expressions [are used] to pander to a sadistic voyeurism among viewers' (ibid.: 262). According to Alcoff and Gray, then, there is a premium on – because there is a 'pleasure' to be had in – the disclosure of women's pain. This prurient interest is, moreover, a mass interest and not the pathetic, pathological interest of a few (men). Kilroy is not the exception but the rule. Here, then, prurient interest appears as the only possible response. By establishing and responding to a peep-show mentality, women's talk-show testimony is packaged as an experience for public vilification and not moral edification. Following the logic set out by Alcoff and Gray, talk shows promote not just a rampant individualism but a distinctly base individualism where viewer self-interest and the pursuit of 'pleasure' knows no limits. Rape used to name a reality of violent injustice; today rape is a word that has general pornographic value. Little wonder, then, that talk shows have become a cipher for political anxiety over the ethical nature of human relations in late modernity, and in so doing have put paid to a simple faith in a cultural politics of trauma.

Offering what is by their own admission a deeply despairing account of media and public interest in women's talk-show testimony and by extension the power of confessional culture, it is not surprising that Alcoff and Gray are keen to look elsewhere for a model of 'transgressive' testimony, and in so doing they offer a glimmer of hope. Indeed, they are keen to maintain the importance of personal testimony, hence they write:

> A project of social change [. . .] does not need to get beyond the personal narrative or the confessional to become political but rather needs to analyse the various effects of the confessional in different contexts and struggle to create discursive spaces in which we can maximise its disruptive effects. (ibid.: 284)

In sum, they assert that: 'We need new ways to analyze the personal and the political as well as new ways to conceptualise these terms' (ibid.).

Critically, Alcoff and Gray start this project when, in stark contrast to the spectacle of women's talk-show disclosures, they offer a surprising counter-example: writing on toilet – or, as they prefer, bathroom – walls. Describing it as a form of 'anonymous accusation' and inspired by a group of students at Brown University, who, following a spate of campus rapes, began listing the names of rapists on the walls of women's bathrooms, Alcoff and Gray argue that 'By not signing such lists and choosing a relatively secluded place in which to write, the women could minimize their own exposure to recrimination' (ibid.: 287). Thus, they argue, 'bathroom lists represent an interesting and innovative attempt to make survivor discourse public in such a way as to minimize the dangers of speaking out for survivors yet maximize the disruptive nature of survivor outrage' (ibid.). Alcoff and Gray's use of bathroom lists – or, as I prefer, toilet graffiti – as an example of the power of women's testimony to sexual violence is a politically imaginative move. It not only feels delightfully subversive but clearly answers the imperatives established by Alcoff and Gray for a radical politics, on the one hand guaranteeing a measure of autonomy and safety for women giving testimony, and on the other guaranteeing institutional uproar which included, in this case, concern over the rights of the named perpetrators, and a frenzy of response and reaction from the university authorities accusing the women of libel, harassment and 'striking against the heart of the American judicial system'. But as Alcoff and Gray note, despite efforts to wipe away the lists, the women kept on writing, and the lists grew from ten names to include thirty. As a consequence the university authorities were forced to strengthen and improve their procedures for dealing with crimes of sexual violence (ibid.: 286–7). And while writing on toilet walls does not normally become 'a target for socio-legal intervention in the way that political slogans [and public graffiti] have been', because it is normally 'conversational' in address and because it is 'public only to the extent that members of the public see it when they use toilet facilities' (Young 2004: 51), the Brown University graffiti is defiantly brilliant in this respect, and as a consequence it carries the possibility of reconfiguring what we understand to be political sloganeering, the powers of conversational address and the constitution of public space.

By giving testimony behind closed doors and thus beyond the reach of a controlling authority, the women were able to retain a measure of their autonomy and thereby control over the content, context, coherency and connections of their speaking and writing. In other words, according to Alcoff and Gray, they resisted the recuperating logic of public confession and gave witness to their reality, which they define as being the power 'to speak out, to name the unnameable, to turn and face it down' (1993). By giving testimony we cease being faceless victims. For Alcoff and Gray, then, the imperative is to give women the opportunity to gain face. It is, of course, a deep paradox that Alcoff and Gray rely on a scenario of anonymity to restore agency to women, a point I shall return to.

For the moment, however, I want to query their definition of witnessing. According to Alcoff and Gray a witness 'knows the truth' of her own experience and is thus capable of naming it despite its being 'unnameable' in the prior instance, thereby figuring the witness with an incredible agency at her disposal, an agency with the power to name that which has an intractable, obdurate status outside language. What is inconceivable to Alcoff and Gray is the idea that traumatic reality might always resist being known and named, which is to say that it remains truly *unnameable*. In other words, what they do not consider is that trauma is 'unnameable' not because it has been suppressed by patriarchal myths (or even the machinations of modern power) but because it remains permanently outside the power of language. Or perhaps more accurately, trauma resists the grasp of language – and with it the grasp of the subject – not because it remains in some space or indeed time outside of discourse but because it has no meaning to offer language. Importantly, for feminists such as Alcoff and Gray the reality of sexual abuse while suppressed and rendered silent by patriarchal discourse remains, nonetheless, full of latent meaning: the meaning of reality. (The same goes for Haug.) The challenge, as I figure it, is to formulate a politics not necessarily reliant on a reality figured as that which *gives* meaning, but rather a politics based on a reality figured as that for which meaning is immaterial or at least an inherent abstraction. This is not a denial of there being 'truth', but rather I am trying to say that the *reality of truth* might be inadequate to the task set it by feminism. In other words, as I see it, the challenge is to establish a model of political testimony based on a language that begins with its own defeat, with defeat as its first principle, yet does not succumb or collapse into the language of defeatism. (Defeat is not a future option, but only ever the place we are moving away from.)

In terms of politics this is a language never happy with itself, always unhappy at what has been said, for the limits of having said. Politics on this model is always (a) work in progress. It never rests, and can never be measured in terms of material success if the latter is thought 'appropriable as a phenomenon of essence'. It is an impossibly talkative politics, a politics talking beyond the strictures of known power, outside the order of intentionality: a radically impersonal, faceless, spectacularly nonphenomenal politics. In light of all this talk, it is time again to listen a little more closely to what exceeds the grasp of women's talk-show testimony, for testimony I am arguing is always an event beyond understanding, and not a representation, a point almost made by Alcoff and Gray, as I shall now argue.

Although accrediting little political significance to talk shows, Alcoff and Gray do acknowledge that 'transgressive moments have occurred on TV talk shows' (1993: 278), whereupon they cite a particular episode of *The Oprah Winfrey Show*. This show was special because, first, Winfrey 'subverted her ability to be a more objective and dispassionate observer of victims on the stage' because of her identification with them, hence she rarely 'allows them to be put in the position of having to defend the truth of their stories or their own actions' (ibid.: 278). Second, coupled with the fact that the audience consisted of about 200 women, nearly all of whom were survivors, the show gave rise to 'a wide-ranging "horizontal" group discussion' with 'little deferral to the designated expert', and this by turn meant that the

> show had the most potential to thwart the efforts to contain and recuperate the disruptive potential of survivor discourse precisely because it could not be contained or segregated within a separate, less threatening realm: there was too much of it for any one expert to handle and the victim–expert split could not be maintained. [. . .] For at least one brief moment on television, survivors were the subjects of their own lives. (ibid.: 279)

While Alcoff and Gray express some optimism here and in so doing go some way to remedy a critique of talk shows which is reliant for its cogency on an (empirically and poorly) imagined viewing public, their language of remedy relies on how closely this particular show approximates the model of consciousness-raising groups and its logic of mutual recognition and identification, as well as the logic of self-authorship. But this is hardly TV. And it is hardly the best model. Indeed, according to Haug, it was already an exhausted model in 1980s. She writes:

> Women [had] gained experience through consciousness-raising groups of retrieving from everyday life itself the means of transcending the everyday [but] there came a point at which we could progress no further. Telling stories became a circular process; no one wanted to listen any more. Hauling ourselves out of the water taught us nothing about flying, but a lot about gravity. As long as our experience was encased within obstinately repetitive gestures, it was impossible to say anything of any consequence [. . .] whose nature could not be deduced from any known body of laws. (Haug et al. 1987: 39)

As Haug so beautifully puts it, in a bid to learn something about flying and to ensure that the giving of testimony ceased being a story foretold it was vital even then to create a new body of laws. Thus she recommended a method in which the experience of one woman was 'pitted against another (ibid.: 56) and women were expected to 'complete the rough sketches' of each other's memories (ibid.: 57). Importantly, as Haug argues, 'empathy, by and large, proved unsuitable as a method; *it stood in the way of knowledge*' (ibid.). Set against this model, Kilroy is looking less like a mockery of the consciousness-raising group, and more like its successor, on which count Mellencamp's prediction might yet be true: daytime talk might still be imagined as the 'electronic syndicated version of consciousness-raising groups of the women's movements'.

Corrine Squire would agree. Acknowledging that it is 'easy to deride' the 'loose concatenation of ideas' and the 'emotional and empirical excesses' that characterise the talk-show format (1997: 102), Squire is nonetheless keen to assert that just because talk shows are based on a loose economy of emotion and meaning, this alone does not change the fact that they can also 'build up a complicated picture of psychological, as well as social and historical relationships', which more importantly it 'does not try to resolve' (ibid.: 109). Importantly, then, for Squire is the idea that the show does not try to – and indeed cannot – contain the complex riot it produces. In other words, its aesthetic holds the key – an aesthetic which Squire summarises as: 'punchy questions; short, clear encapsulations of arguments and feelings; brief passages of incoherent speech, tears, or silence to signal deep emotion; bursts of laughter and applause, snatches of theme music bracketing breaks and the programme itself' (ibid.). 'These characteristics', Squire adds, 'produce a currency of rapid, intense, simple, and repetitive aural and visual representations, from the six-note sequence that means *Oprah*, to the screwed-up, crying faces of incest survivors asked "How did it feel?"', and as such they break up 'the coherency and continuity of the talk show's narrative of psychological improvement' (ibid.).

Developing a notion of super-realism to describe this aesthetic, Squire goes on to argue that:

Daytime talk shows like *Oprah* try to reach a realist truth by inter-leaving information and entertainment, and deploying narratives of psychological growth to pull this infotainment together. Sometimes, they do not manage the integration and super-realism, a realism torn out of shape by the excesses of emotion or empiricism, disrupts the explanatory framework. (ibid.)

On *Oprah*, Squire argues, this disruption happens in two ways. First, she suggests 'super-realism may take over when a 'psychological' truth recurs so often on the show that it begins to shed its individual psychological character and starts to look more like a social, political or religious fact'. So, for example, she adds the narratives of sexual abuse on *Oprah* are 'very similar and endlessly repeated', yet they 'seem to go beyond psychological understanding to become facts about gender relationships that demand explanation in other, social terms. It is the televisual superficiality and facility of the show that allows this super-real excess to register' (ibid.: 109–10). Oprah's second type of super-realism, according to Squire's analysis,

> appears when the emotions in the show get so intense that the show forgoes any claim to provide information and simply displays an extreme effect – accessible to psychoanalytic interpretation, perhaps, but not to the kinds of psychological explanations most of us are familiar with and use. (ibid.: 110)

So, for instance, she argues,

> when the show featured an abused woman with 92 personalities, it could not provide a coherent account of her subjectivity. Abuse started to seem utterly idiosyncratic and affectively overwhelming. Again, this registering of excess relied on the show's super-real tele-visual character: on snappy formulations of monstrous feelings and quick moves to commercial breaks ('back in a moment') that left the unspeakable and the unimaginable resounding around American living rooms. (ibid.)

What is interesting about Squire's reading of the transgressive quality of women speaking out about sexual abuse is that it works because the women do not retain control over their words. Their tes-timony is transgressive because they are *not* the subjects of their own lives. Put differently, it works because it is superficial, its meaning is left unsaid by the women. In other words, Squire finds political significance in the fact that no personal meaning can be attached to the subject or her experience, hence leaving it 'unspeakable' and 'unimaginable', whereas for Alcoff and Gray the survivors on *Oprah* became the subjects of their lives on the condition that they are getting their testimony across. In other words, for Alcoff and Gray, the truth was too much for any one expert, thereby the women were given their opportunity to tell it as it is without distorting, mediating influence: the message is sent loud and clear. This is not the logic at work for Squire. Quite the contrary: for her it is impossible to tell it as it is in anyway that is loud *and* clear, precisely because when something becomes overwhelmingly repetitive it exhausts the structures of conventional meaning and, indeed, the structures of personality. There is a logic of repetition and proliferation here that is interesting; if repeated enough, if prolific enough, the message will be heard in its undoing of logic. At the point of proliferation, silence becomes – if not actually meaningful – a resounding truth.

While I do not want to turn silence into a political fetish, there is nonetheless potential here, which is why I am a little disappointed that Squire concludes by arguing that super-realism only has 'some modest feminist value' which is suspended somewhere between 'fluff and gravity' (ibid.: 109, 110). For as far as I am concerned the challenge posed by talk shows is not a question of 'relative' value, but a question of altering the very field of our thinking. This certainly was the challenge recognised by Haug, when she argued that 'it was impossible to say anything of any consequence [. . .] whose nature could not be deduced from any known body of laws'. So, while it might be counterintuitive to figure the *power* of women's testimony as *immaterial*, I think it is a start.

Initially Alcoff and Gray offered women's graffiti as an example of transgressive testimony – in contrast to women's talk-show testimony – yet what they fail to comment on is that the controversy caused by the women's graffiti at Brown University became the topic of a *Phil Donahue Show*, a point they marginalise as a footnote. Conceptually, then, it does not make sense to separate the two examples. Indeed, I want to argue that theoretically they are less distinct and their differences less pronounced than Alcoff and Gray are willing to acknowledge – on at least two key points. First, women's graffiti and talk-show testimony both function according to a logic of anonymity: the women on talk shows, while exposed to view are, in reality, no more known to us than the women hidden from our view. Despite the intimacy and provocation of their address, they remain women without initial or signature. Testimony does not produce us as a community of intimates. Indeed, to my mind, the address of the women on *Kilroy* carries the force of provocation and address because they are unknown to us: they offer us no right of reply and no guarantee of community – or rather the community they offer us is one that is not necessarily built on common ground but the impersonality of a mechanical network. It is a community without known relation.

Hence, while I might understand the impulse, I am, in fact, wary of Alcoff and Gray's attempt to restore 'face' to Tracey, which they do by repeating her name for us, to make her a person in her own right – since in claiming her as one of us, we make her in our likeness. It is fundamentally presumptive, for how can we know what she wants from us, or what recognition she seeks? 'The "face" of the other', Butler argues in her reading of Emmanuel Levinas, 'cannot be read for a secret meaning, and the imperative it delivers is not immediately translatable into a prescription that might be linguistically formulated and followed' (2004a: 131). The 'face, strictly speaking, does not speak' (ibid.: 132). The face of Tracey speaks without speaking to us, we hear her loud and clear without her having to word it out for us in a language we can grasp.

> The face, if we are to put words to its meaning, will be that for which no words really work; the face seems to be a kind of sound, the sound of language evacuating its sense, the sonorous substratum of vocalisation that precedes and limits the delivery of any semantic sense. (ibid.: 135)

In other words, the meaning of 'Tracey's' face is not in her name, but 'in' this nameless challenge to which we are bound without knowing why and for what purpose. If we give her a name, a personality, we can only do so on the basis of what we know of these things; in giving us her name Alcoff and Gray have already cancelled her provocation.

So while in her exposure she might be asking for recognition, 'the challenge is not to substitute the recogniser for the recognised' (ibid.: 48).

Theoretically women's talk-show testimony and toilet testimony are less distinct and their differences less pronounced for a second, related reason: namely they are both subject to a process of constant erasure and proliferation. The memory and reality of women's talk-show testimony does not last from one day to the next, let alone one week to the next, but rather it is subject to a constant turnover. Neither graffiti nor on-air testimony can achieve permanent status, yet this state of constant disappearing becomes the condition for endless possibility for rewriting, for scratching the surface of language again, to figure what the challenge to politics is again. Women's testimony is not as potent as Armstrong once hoped, but nor is it as impotent as some consider. This alone does not signal the end of writing – on the contrary it allows for a certain freedom at both a personal and political level, an opportunity to recast the language of politics, find new measures of knowledge. Usefully, then, we might do well to remember that radical feminism came into being by posing a fundamental challenge to the norms of political analysis. Indeed, in her groundbreaking 'The Feminist Standpoint', Nancy Hartsock took some of her key insights from Marx, but she also sought to subvert the parameters of historical materialism by insisting on the importance of women's experience of domestic work. Key among her examples is a scene taken from Marilyn French's *The Women's Room* in which the protagonist gains a profound insight into her world and into the world of men and their actions when she is cleaning the toilet. By focusing on this politically insignificant, seeming irrelevant, meaningless act, Hartsock was able to argue how women's experiences – in this instance the performing of invisible, uninspiring labour outside the arena of public work and the market economy of exchange value – could not be accommodated by the concepts that had shaped historical materialism. Radical feminism and a politics of women's experiences and testimony were born. Notwithstanding all the criticisms that have been made of Hartsock's work, her achievement, and the achievement of radical feminism more generally, was a testing of the limits of what could count as politically meaningful, of what could count as historical, material evidence of oppression and suffering. In short, Hartsock sought to challenge what constituted the political 'real' and how a claim could be made on the 'real' of the political – by pointing to something seemingly outrageous. Haug, in some respects, is attempting to reverse the claim on the real by once more trying to re-establish the primacy of economic measures. But rather than have recourse to the logic of radical feminism – which would look to reassert the primacy of women's personal experiences and testimony, as Alcoff and Gray do by looking to site politics back in the privacy afforded by toilets – what I have been trying to do is hold open the space in which momentarily Haug struggled to articulate a response when she first saw the women crying on TV and the space in which she struggled to understand the women in the classroom. For I am not sure that we yet know, if we can ever know, why women cry on TV and who they are when they speak.

What I am pushing for is a politics that is not based on the guaranteed promise of change but on the promise of change as contingent possibility, and thus freeing politics from relying on an economy of appearance and permanence. What I am hoping for is an understanding of testimony not reliant on an economy of signature, and as a consequence raising I hope what is perhaps the key question here, namely what constitutes a lasting record. Twenty-seven years after her appearance on *The Today Show*, there is, of course, no record of Armstrong's testimony, nor is there any record of the women on *Kilroy*. Quite literally they were on air one minute, off air the next, the record of their appearance and appeal to others instantly wiped clean. Whatever difference they made was made in the event of speaking, an incalculable difference. The same stands for every minute women continue to give on-air testimony. This disappearance of women's testimony, and with it an entire economy of political meaning, is not simply a function of the talk-show format, as Armstrong maintains, but a function also of the trauma that violence inflicts on language. Trauma disappears from testimony and, while this might be a source of frustration for critics, I would argue that it offers a politics that has to keep renewing its commitment to writing, which I consider a good thing. To sum up, then, in response to the fact that the Brown University authorities kept on cleaning the graffiti off the toilet walls, one of the women responsible for writing the lists left a message asking, somewhat innocently, 'Who erased all the names?' To this another woman responded, but not quite in answer, 'Don't let this get washed away. Fight!' Write!

Bibliography

Alcoff, L. and L. Gray (1993), 'Survivor discourse: transgression or recuperation', *SIGNS: Journal of Women in Culture and Society*, 18:2, 260–90.

Armstrong, L. (1978), *Kiss Daddy Goodnight*, London and New York: Pocket.

Armstrong, L. (1987), *Kiss Daddy Goodnight: Ten Years Later*, London and New York: Pocket.

Armstrong, L. (1994), *Rocking the Cradle of Sexual Politics: What Happened When Women Said Incest*, London: The Women's Press.

Bass, E. and L. Davis (1988), *The Courage to Heal*, London: Mandarin.

Bass, E. and L. Thornton (1993), *I Never Told Anyone*, London: Harper-Perennial.

Bennett, J. (2005), *Empathic Vision: Affect, Trauma, and Contemporary Art*, Stanford, CA: Stanford University Press.

Brison, S. (2002), *Aftermath: Violence and the Remaking of the Self*, Princeton: Princeton University Press.

Brown, W. (1995), *States of Injury: Power and Freedom in Late Modernity*, Princeton, NJ: Princeton University Press.

Butler, J. (2004a), *Precarious Life: The Powers of Violence and Mourning*, London: Verso.

Butler, J. (2004b), 'Quandaries of the Incest Taboo', in J. Butler, *Undoing Gender*, London and New York: Routledge.

Campbell, S. (2003), *Relational Remembering: Rethinking the Memory Wars*, Oxford: Rowman and Littlefield.

Caruth, C. (ed.) (1995), *Trauma: Explorations in Memory*, Baltimore and London: Johns Hopkins University Press.

Caruth, C. (1996), *Unclaimed Experience*, Baltimore and London: Johns Hopkins University Press.

Clegg, C. (1999), 'Feminist recoveries in *My Father's House*', *Feminist Review*, 61: 67–87.

Crews, F. (1995), *The Memory Wars: Freud's Legacy in Dispute*, London: Granta.

Culbertson, R. (1995), 'Embodied memory, transcendence, and telling: recounting trauma, re-establishing the self', *New Literary History*, 26: 169–75.

Cvetkovich, A. (2003), *An Archive of Feelings: Trauma, Sexuality, and Lesbian Public Cultures*, Durham and London: Duke University Press.

Dardenne, S., with Marie-Thérèse Cuny (2004), *I Choose To Live*, trans. P. Dening, London: Virago.

Douglass, A. and T. A. Vogler (eds) (2003), *Witness and Memory: The Discourse of Trauma*, London and New York: Routledge.

Elsaesser, T. (2001), 'Postmodernism as mourning work', *Screen*, 42: 2, 199–201.

Felman, S. (2002), *The Juridical Unconscious: Trials and Trauma in the Twentieth Century*, Cambridge, MA: Harvard University Press.

Felman, S. and D. Laub (1992), *Testimony: Crises of Witnessing in Literature, Psychoanalysis and History*, London and New York: Routledge.

Foster, H. (1996), *The Return of the Real*, Cambridge, MA: MIT Press.

Fraser, S. (1987), *My Father's House: A Memoir of Incest and of Healing*, London: Virago.

Gilmore, L. (2001), *The Limits of Autobiography: Trauma and Testimony*, Ithaca and London: Cornell University Press.

Hacking, I. (1994), 'Memoro-politics, trauma and the soul', *History of the Human Sciences*, 7: 2, 29–52.

Hacking, I. (1995), *Rewriting the Soul: Multiple Personality and the Sciences of Memory*, Princeton, NJ: Princeton University Press.

Haraway, D. (1991), 'The cyborg manifesto: science, technology, and socialist-feminism in the late twentieth century', in D. Haraway, *Simians, Cyborg and Women: The Reinvention of Nature*, London: Free Association.

Hartman, G. (1995), 'On traumatic knowledge and literary studies', *New Literary History*, 2: 537–63.

Hartsock, N. (1987), 'The feminist standpoint: developing the ground for a specifically feminist historical materialism', in S. Harding (ed.), *Feminism and Methodology*, Bloomington and Indianapolis: Indiana University Press.

Haug, F. (2001), 'Sexual deregulation, or, the child abuser as hero in neoliberalism', *Feminist Theory*, 2: 1, 55–78.

Haug, F. et al. (1987), *Female Sexualization: A Collective Work of Memory*, trans. E. Carter, London: Verso.

Heart, K. F. H. (1991), 'Womon throwing off rage', in L. M. Wisechild (ed.), *She Who Is Lost Is Remembered: Healing from Incest through Creativity*, Washington: Seal.

Henke, S. A. (1998), *Shattered Subjects: Trauma and Testimony in Women's Writing*, Basingstoke and London: Macmillan.

Herman, J. Lewis, (1992), *Trauma and Recovery: From Domestic Abuse to Political Terror*, London: Pandora.

King, N. (2000), *Memory, Narrative, Identity*, Edinburgh: Edinburgh University Press.

LaCapra, D. (2000), *History and Reading: Tocqueville, Foucault, French Studies*, Toronto: University of Toronto Press.

Laub, D. (1995), 'Truth and testimony: the process and the struggle', in C. Caruth (ed.), *Trauma: Explorations in Memory*, Baltimore and London: Johns Hopkins University Press.

Luckhurst, R. (2003), 'Traumaculture', *New Formations*, 50: 40–61.

Mardorossian, C. (2002), 'Toward a new feminist theory of rape', *Signs. Journal of Women in Culture and Society*, 27: 3, 743–75.

Marstine, J. (2002), 'Challenging the gendered categories of art and art therapy: the paintings of Jane Orleman', *Feminist Studies*, 28: 3, 631–54.

Martinez, B. (1991), 'Incest: "Show and Tell" ', in L. M. Wisechild (ed.), *She Who Is Lost Is Remembered: Healing from Incest through Creativity*, Washington: Seal.

Masson, J. (1984), *The Assault on Truth: Freud and Child Sexual Abuse*, London: Fontana.

Miller, A. (1990), *The Untouched Key: Tracing Childhood Trauma in Creativity and Destructiveness*, London: Virago.

Mowitt, J. (2000), 'Trauma envy', *Cultural Critique*, 46.

Ness, L. (1991) 'The art of survival', in L. M. Wisechild (ed.), *She Who Is Lost Is Remembered: Healing from Incest through Creativity*, Washington: Seal.

Newall, K. (1991), 'My body's language', in L. M. Wisechild (ed.), *She Who Is Lost Is Remembered: Healing from Incest through Creativity*, Washington: Seal.

Pollock, G. (2001), *Looking Back to the Future: Essays on Art, Life and Death*, B&G Arts International: Amsterdam.

Radstone, S. (1999), 'Review article: Elaine Showalter, *Hystories: Hysterical Epidemics and Modern Culture*', in K. L. Rogers, S. Leydesdorff and G. Dawson (eds), *Trauma and Life Stories: International Perspectives*, London and New York: Routledge.

Radstone, S. (2000), 'Screening trauma: Forrest Gump, film and memory', in S. Radstone (ed.), *Memory and Methodology*, Oxford and New York: Berg.

Reavey, P. and S. Warner (eds) (2003), *New Feminist Stories of Child Sexual*

Abuse: Sexual Scripts and Dangerous Dialogues, London and New York: Routledge.

Ronell, A. (1994), 'Video/television/Rodney King: twelve steps beyond the pleasure principle', in G. Bender and T. Druckrey (eds), *Culture on the Brink: Ideologies of Technology*, Seattle: Bay.

Rooney, E. (1996), 'What's the story? Feminist theory, narrative, address', *differences: A Journal of Feminist Cultural Studies*, 8: 1, 1–30.

Rothberg, M. (2000), *Traumatic Realism: The Demands of Holocaust Representation*, Minnesota: University of Minnesota.

Scott, A. (1988), 'Feminism and the seductiveness of the "real event"', *Feminist Review*, 28: 88–102.

Seltzer, M. (1998), *Serial Killers: Death and Life in America's Wound Culture*, London and New York: Routledge.

Shattuc, J. (1997), *The Talking Cure: TV Talk Shows and Women*, London and New York: Routledge.

Showalter, E. (1997), *Hystories: Hysterical Epidemics and Modern Culture*, London: Picador.

Squire, C. (1997), 'Empowering women? The *Oprah Winfrey Show*', in C. Brunsdon, J. D' Acci and L. Spigel (eds), *Feminist Television Criticism*, Oxford: Clarendon.

Tal, K. (1996), *Worlds of Hurt: Reading the Literatures of Trauma*, Cambridge: Cambridge University Press.

Young, A. (2004), *Judging the Image: Art, Value, Law*, London and New York: Routledge.

Young, D. (1996), 'Remembering trouble: three lives, three stories', in P. Antze and M. Lambek (eds), *Tense Past: Cultural Essays on Memory*, London and New York: Routledge.

Winkler, C. (2002), *One Night: Realities of Rape*, Walnut Creek, CA: AltaMira.

Wisechild, L. M. (ed.) (1991), *She Who Is Lost Is Remembered: Healing from Incest through Creativity*, Washington: Seal.

Index